VINCENT'S

1863–2013

Dear Stanislas,

with fond remories
of your oxford trip.

Simon Lee

THIRD MILLENNIUM
PUBLISHING, LONDON

Vincent's 1863–2013

© Vincent's Appeal Trust Company, 2014

Design and compilation © Third Millennium Information Ltd

First published in 2014 by Third Millennium Publishing Ltd,
a subsidiary of Third Millennium Information Ltd.

2–5 Benjamin Street
London
United Kingdom
EC1M 5QL

www.tmiltd.com

ISBN 978 1 908990 33 4

Text by Simon Lee
Designed by Matthew Wilson
Production by Bonnie Murray
Printed by Gorenjski Tisk, Slovenia

Contents

List of Plates

Picture acknowledgments:
PA   Press Association
28   Oxford University Images
39   British Pathé
70   5th Avenue Digital/FFL Partners
All others © Vincent's Club, Oxford

Acknowledgments

I am most grateful to Sir Roger Bannister for his generous words, and especially his wise observation about the relevance of Edmund Burke's point that a society is a covenant between generations. Melville Guest and Chris Atkinson from the Vincent's 150 Committee first invited me to speak and then to write about the history of their Club. I would like to thank them for this opportunity, for their patience and their encouragement, and I also extend those thanks to the current and recent officers of Vincent's who welcomed me into the Club and answered my questions freely, especially Marcus-Alexander Neil, Ben Mansfield, Adam Healy (all Presidents), Stephen Eeley, the Bursar, and Simon Offen, the V150 Administrator. Various members attending functions in the UK and South Africa offered perceptive comments. I would also like to thank Andrew Thomas, now of St Peter's College but then Head of Sports Development at the University, who invited me to write and speak about the history of Oxford sportsmen and sportswomen, which brought my interest to the attention of Vincent's. Dr John Hood, a Vincent's member, Chair of the Rhodes Trustees and formerly Vice-Chancellor of the University of Oxford, introduced me to Dr Sarah Thomas, Bodley's Librarian, who in turn ensured that I had access to the Proctors' File and other material held by the Bodleian. In the detective work necessary to identify who was and was not a member, the early lists held by the Bodleian were invaluable, as was the assistance of the library staff at every stage. Julian Platt, Joel Burden, Christopher Fagg, Matt Wilson and colleagues at Third Millennium have been exemplary in turning the text into this book. The Third Millennium team, Melville Guest and Chris Atkinson have been particularly assiduous in selecting photographs.

Inevitably, many members and other readers will be prompted by this book to draw attention to other photos and to the stories of other Vincent's characters. It would also be helpful if any corrections or further information about members could be sent to the Club. By the 200th anniversary, if not before, Vincent's deserves to have a full list of its membership since 1863. At every point in the book, many more examples of members could have been given, so I ask for tolerance and forgiveness where others would have preferred different themes and illustrations. The intention has been not to have the last word in a comprehensive account year by year, person by person, but simply to capture something of the spirit of this remarkable Club and its extraordinary range of Oxford students over 150 years. In that endeavour, there might be some points of relevance to a wider readership interested in education, undergraduate-led societies, clubs more generally, sport, character and fellowship.

Simon Lee
January 2014

Foreword

SIR ROGER BANNISTER

In 1955, I wrote briefly of the mysterious institution called Vincent's, feeling myself to be supremely unclubbable, quaking with nervousness on entering the Club, having a veneration for the Club's tradition and of later finding it to be one of Oxford's most enjoyable institutions. I was first taken there by Sir Tommy Macpherson and felt it was an honour to be elected to membership and then to become president and indeed to have a room there. As has been widely noted, my friends and I repaired to Vincent's from the Iffley Road track on 6 May 1954 and I have greatly enjoyed its fellowship ever since.

The founder of Vincent's, W B Woodgate, has remained to many of us a particular mystery. The opening and concluding chapters of this book do much to explain the genius of this great rower. It is of special interest to me to see how he was both the founder of an enduring society in Vincent's yet he was himself rather 'unclubbable'. Although Simon Lee is generous to my own generation – the middle 50 years of this 150 year story – I have enjoyed just as much the way in which he retrieves the early history of the Club's pioneers and celebrates the latest half-century of high-flyers.

Having heard Simon Lee speak at an Oxford alumni weekend in 2011 on Oxford's Olympians, I was pleased that Vincent's asked him to write a history of our Club. Lord Butler hosted a particularly friendly dinner at the House of Lords in 2012 when Simon Lee spoke specifically about Vincent's Olympians. Now, in 2014, we have this book by him which ranges more broadly and I commend it to members and to all who care about our sporting and educational institutions. Likewise, I also applaud the fund-raising efforts by the Vincent's 150 Committee which have in a sense re-founded the Club so it may flourish for the next 150 years and beyond.

Finally, to borrow from Edmund Burke's famous observation about the nature of society, I see Vincent's as 'a partnership, not only between those who are living but between those who are living, those who are dead and those who are yet to be born'.

CHAPTER I

The Founder:
W B Woodgate (1841–1920)

WB Woodgate, the founder of Vincent's, was the W G Grace of rowing. That was the judgment of Steve Fairbairn who was Australia's and Cambridge's answer in the 20th century to Woodgate's pre-eminence in the 19th century as a rowing coach, writer and critic. Himself an outstanding rower in the latter decades of the 19th century, Fairbairn had benefited personally from Woodgate's coaching. Fairbairn's own standing in the sport is shown by the tribute to him on the Putney course – the famous Mile Post obelisk. His letter in November 1920 to *The Field* magazine on Woodgate's death reflects on the great man's influence:

> In 1881, when I first came to England, Woodgate stood in much the same position in the rowing world that W G Grace occupied in the cricket world. At Henley this year I had many rowing chats with him, and his judgment on a crew or an individual was as unerringly correct as ever … I always had the greatest admiration for him, and feel that as an oar, a coach or a critic of rowing, his loss is irreparable.

Fairbairn's judgment is supported by the *The University Boat Race Official Centenary History* compiled in 1929 by G C Drinkwater MC (OUBC) and T R B Sanders (CUBC), edited and with an introduction by His Honour Judge C Gurdon (CUBC). This is as imposing and impartial an account as can be found, given the august occasion of its publication, the reputation of its writers and the two-to-one ratio of Cambridge to Oxford men in the editorial crew. Their judgment is unequivocal, drawing on Woodgate's performances at Henley as well as his part in two victories in the Boat Race itself, by 30 seconds in 1862 and by 45 seconds in 1863:

> W B Woodgate made his first appearance this year. His rowing career was the most remarkable of all. He entered in 1862 for the Stewards', Visitors', Goblets, and Diamonds, won the first three and dead-heated in the last-named … An

encyclopaedia of knowledge, he never used his faculties to gain wealth or fame, but he wrote much on rowing … No one has been more sadly missed from the riverside than 'Guts' since his death soon after the war at the age of eighty, and few men have had apter nicknames than he.

Nor was it simply in 1862 that Woodgate was victorious at Henley. He won the Goblets in 1861 and again in 1862 when he also held the Wingfield sculls as well as the Stewards' and Visitors'. In 1863, he won the Goblets again. In 1864, it was the Diamonds and the Wingfield sculls. In 1865, he won the Grand Challenge Cup, in 1866, the Goblets, in 1867 the Wingfield sculls and, in 1868, the Goblets.

Meanwhile, his Oxford sequence, in addition to the two victories in the Boat Race, was also remarkable. In 1860, 1861 and 1862 he won the OUBC Pairs with three different partners, who each went on to become clergymen, Revd H F Baxter, Canon Champneys and Revd R Shepherd. In 1861 and 1862 he won the OUBC sculls. In 1863 he had the joy of combining Oxford and Henley, winning with Brasenose, defeating Trinity Hall, Cambridge.

When Woodgate, in his last year as an undergraduate, founded Vincent's Club in 1863, his vision was to bring together Oxford's leading 100 sportsmen and all-round characters. Vincent's, in Woodgate's own phrase, 'at once acquired a special prestige, which has never left it'. He wanted the Club to last at least until its Jubilee, its 50th anniversary, and to live long enough to witness that himself. Both wishes were fulfilled. Woodgate died in 1920, at the age of 80. Vincent's proceeded to its centenary, when the main speaker at the celebratory dinner was the Prime Minister of the day, Harold Macmillan. Famous Vincent's alumni included Macmillan's successor as Prime Minister later that year, Alec Douglas-Home, and sportsmen such as the Olympian gold medal winner and king of Norway, Olav V. Now that Vincent's is celebrating its 150th anniversary, it is timely to begin reflecting on the Club and its members by recovering an understanding, which earlier generations would have acquired directly or by word of mouth, of the kind of person the founder was.

The short answer is given by the heading to his obituary in *The Times* in November 1920: 'Sportsman and Bohemian'.

One long answer, running to over 500 pages, was given by Walter Bradford Woodgate himself, 11 years earlier, in his *Reminiscences of an Old Sportsman*. Even in such a tome, he does not discuss his own Blues and countless successes at Henley. Instead, Woodgate gives handsome thanks to his teachers and fellow-students at Radley, Brasenose and the rest of Oxford. His love of good fellowship shines through a rag-bag of amusing anecdotes and trenchant opinions.

On Woodgate as a sportsman, the judgment of all observers in his lifetime and on his death was unanimously positive. On Woodgate as a person, the *Oxford Dictionary of National Biography* is generous:

> Woodgate was a man of unflinching rectitude, of decided opinions, but also of great kindliness, and he was an excellent raconteur. As a young man he was strikingly handsome; in later years his fine, stern face and stalwart figure made him a typical John Bull, an effect accentuated by a low-crowned top hat.

Woodgate had his hats made to a design of his own. This was his way in life more generally. *The Times* in its obituary emphasised his originality and the way his gift for friendship spanned the generations:

> His contemporaries or, perhaps one should say, his coevals, recognised him as an original character, for not only did they treasure stories of his eccentricities, but they invented them. He himself laughed at many, and his friends laughed at many more which he never heard.

It is not easy to separate the facts from the legends, but the former begin with his birth in 1840 to Maria Woodgate (née Bradford, hence his middle name) and her husband Canon Henry A Woodgate. W B does not tell us in a straightforward way that he was one of nine but he mentions three older sisters and five younger brothers, one of whom in particular he revered, General Sir Edward Woodgate, who was killed in action in the Boer War in 1900.

Nor does he explain almost anything about his mother or, for instance, the Oxford form of his father, although he mentions in an aside his father's First Class Honours in Greats and the treats he had of visits to the University as a child through his father's connections. In 1838, Canon Woodgate, a Fellow of St John's, had given the prestigious Bampton Lectures in the University of Oxford, which he dedicated on publication in 1839 to his great friend, John Henry (later Cardinal, now Blessed) Newman. W B Woodgate does mention that Newman was godfather to one of W B's sisters, and that another distinguished Anglican turned Catholic, Henry (also later Cardinal) Manning, was one of W B Woodgate's own godfathers.

Woodgate is at pains to tell us in the opening pages of his memoir that he can recall details of his childhood from before the age of two. Others would doubt whether that is possible, although his later feats on the water, recorded for posterity in the annals of Henley, veer towards the improbable yet true. Until he went to Radley at the age of ten, he studied at home in the Belbroughton rectory in Worcestershire with his older sisters and their governess. But he was allowed to run errands on a pony from an early age, learning to ride at the age of seven. He had considerable freedom, and used to take the opportunity to ride to the county borders when he heard of a prize-fight. The older people watching and betting on these bouts looked after the little boy who was thrilled to shake the hand of a boxing champion. When he was eight, he was taught by his father's groom how to ride a horse over fences, with an eye to the light boy being an appropriate jockey for an old horse, and duly won his first race, unbeknown to his parents. Betting, although not by Woodgate as a little boy, was never far from such fights or races. In adulthood, Woodgate put into practice what he had learned about gambling, although he could, he tells us, go two or three days without having a wager. As a student at the University, he was not afraid of boxing or of betting or, it seems, of anything. He enjoyed the outdoors and adventure. His strong memories of childhood were of always having been fascinated by the water.

From before he went to school, then, this vicar's son mixed with all-comers, from the crowds around prize-fights to prelates and politicians. As a child, for example, he knew, as friends of his parents' friends, the Gladstones. Stories about him, and by him, show that he could see the goodness in the unfortunate, even in the rogues, and as a student onwards, he drew attention to the absurdities in the most privileged. He reserved the tolerance of the unconventional that is suggested by 'Bohemian' for the big issues of lifestyle, where others were not being disadvantaged. On relatively petty matters, in contrast, he took great exception to people trying to take a liberty through pilfering or deception or the imposition of unmerited charges. College scouts, 'court underlings' and railway porters all incurred his wrath in this regard, even though he was a staunch friend of scouts in other respects and was moved by the enthusiasm with which, at their own expense, they would follow their students' endeavours at Henley.

Woodgate abhorred the railway companies that exploited their passengers. He disliked proctors, stewards and any others in authority who were pompous and overweening. He had a great generosity of spirit, however, when it came to his sporting opponents. He enjoyed their company in the immediate aftermath of contests and became firm friends with many. He could even warm, over a glass or more, to a proctor or steward or, if they were paying for his dinner, to a railway company.

There is one prejudice of his time that would make his *Reminiscences* unpalatable in this century, and that is his tone and language in describing people of different ethnic origins, and in relating stories in that spirit by others, such as Dr Livingstone. The same approach features in another, younger, Oxford sportsman and writer of note, Sir Theodore Cook. If there is any saving grace in Woodgate's memoirs on this unedifying matter, he did recognise the limitations of his lack of travel. He had only once been to a foreign country, when rowing at the Paris international regatta:

> I always regret that I have not travelled more. I should have opened and improved
> my mind by seeing more of the outside world. But, if I did travel, I should elect
> for Mesopotamia, India and Colonies – and US – and let the European continent
> slide. So far Paris and Rouen have been my limits of view over-sea: not counting
> Ireland in the latter sense, it being part of our realm.

To understand how his other views were formed, it is necessary to understand his experiences at school. In 1850, at the age of ten, Woodgate went to board at Radley, a school that was even younger than he was. He was deeply impressed by the culture fostered by the founder of Radley, Warden Sewell, who originally installed others as the first two heads of the school but who took on the headship himself during Woodgate's time there. Sewell disliked tutors behaving as spies, identifying miscreants. He preferred to trust the boys to live up to responsibility. Woodgate absorbed this lesson. As an undergraduate, he took a stern view against the actions, for example, of 'Wasty' Wade, a don in the lower reaches of the proctors' offices, who went in disguise to Witney on the trail of badly behaved students. Woodgate was fully behind those who shamed Wade at a graduation in the Sheldonian shortly afterwards.

To describe the impact of Sewell's trust on the boys, Woodgate deploys in his book of *Reminiscences* what has become to us a cliché: poacher turned gamekeeper. But in Woodgate's case, he really knew what he was talking about when using this metaphor. As a schoolboy at Radley he had set wires in the woods, caught pheasants and gathered his haul under cover of darkness before waylaying the carrier before 6am, and consigning a brace, addressed to himself, as if from a parent or patron. Although he feared that the dead birds would still be warm and not stiff, matron never tumbled this ruse or, at least, never let on if she did. But when he was made a prefect's assistant, a 'senior inferior', young Woodgate voluntarily gave up this practice.

He learned from one of his teachers, Revd H Gibbings, the value of memorising huge chunks of Greek and Latin, which impressed the writers of his obituaries 70 years later. He was not oblivious to the defects of the school. In particular, he was conscious of being underfed and overtired. The diet and the hours allowed for sleep were simply insufficient. Anticipating by more than 150 years the interest of modern athletes and coaches in nutrition and the importance of rest, he blamed Radley for having stunted his growth. His lack of weight accounts for his slow entry into the leading crews at Radley and Oxford.

He was always game for a challenge. As a schoolboy, on a springy wooden flooring in a cloister, measured at exactly 80 yards, Woodgate took on the task of eating two whole pots of jam and then running up and down 100 times within an hour. He managed it easily. He dispensed with bread as wasting time and ate the jam with a spoon from the jars. He reckoned that the springiness of the wood added about 10 per cent to his pace but, even so, nine miles at an average of less than six and a half minutes was an impressive feat of endurance for a relatively malnourished boy.

His first efforts in a boat came in 1853 when he had passed the swimming test required as a safety measure by Radley. His partner in the boat was Albert Eden Seymour, with whom he rowed in the victorious Oxford crew in the 1864 Boat Race. There was, however, much competition from the older boys for the best boats, so W B Woodgate, ever the lateral thinker, took out the least fashionable boat on his own, a 'Wager' wherry which was very difficult to control and thus unpopular. This is how he came to master the art of sculling and the wider craft of what he called 'aquatics'.

Size being against him, it was only in his last year, 1858, that he made the Radley eight, but that was the year of their private challenge to the established leaders in schoolboy rowing, Eton, to a race at Henley (and, as a practice, a race against an Oxford college crew). Woodgate judges that he was the worst oar in the boat, which lost by only a small margin to Eton. One of the other members of the Radley crew, John Xavier Merriman, was later premier of the Cape in South Africa.

Sir Theodore Cook wrote that,

> His first crew was the Radley eight of 1856, in which he rowed six, and was coached by Bishop MacRorie, who rowed head of the river for Brasenose. The boys easily beat a scratch crew from Oxford with four Blues in it (and six BNC oarsmen), and little Woodgate's weight (he was only just sixteen) was 7st 6lb. He grew into a splendid figure of a man soon afterwards.

When training for that first race at Henley, Woodgate had spent a week in Oxford taking the entrance examinations for Brasenose, where Radley had a strong rowing connection. To keep his place in the Radley boat, he took the train back and forth each late afternoon, but he did well in his papers earlier each day and won an open scholarship to read Greats. He was too young to go into residence that year, but the original intention of going up in Michaelmas 1859 was deemed, on reflection, to leave him too long a time back at school. This is why he started at Brasenose, rather oddly, in *January* 1859.

He was known there initially as Dove, partly in reference to his 'childlike complexion' and partly to the motto of Radley, which includes '*sicut columbae*' (meaning as gentle 'as doves', preceded by '*sicut serpentes*', meaning as wise 'as serpents'). Woodgate explains that, 'I was very effeminate in appearance'. This in turn won him a part in a college play as Lady Barbara when a more established student fell ill. In case anyone missed his triumphant performance in the play, he proceeded to celebrate in hall afterwards, while still in make-up and costume, to such an extent that everyone in college remembered him as Lady Barbara. Some rowing chums still only called him by that name decades later. Eventually, however, he acquired the nickname 'Guts', a reference primarily to his heroic character as a rower and sculler, possibly with the slightest of affectionate allusions also to the blossoming figure of later caricature. But it was in the straightforward sense of having immense courage that the Boat Race historians recorded the aptness of 'Guts' to capture the essence of W B Woodgate.

Nevertheless, he was simply not big enough to make the university crew in his first two years: 'I was but half grown then: scaling well under 10st (9st 10lb, I think).' In life before lightweight crews, the solution was simple and undertaken by Woodgate with gusto: 'The training was old-fashioned and barbarous; raw steaks and a run round the "parks" before morning chapel.' We know that he was putting on weight but was still 'well under 10st 7lb' at the end of term when he won an 'open hack race ... over the Wendlebury course'. Other evidence of his youthful appearance comes from his story of complaining to Tester, the High Street fishmonger, about the smell of his lobster-boiling, which made Woodgate's rooms 'odoriferous': 'Tester patronisingly stroked my infantile cheeks with a fishy paw, and bade me "Go home to your Mammy".' The tradesman was forced by the College to apologise in person. Woodgate's ability to make friendships out of unpromising encounters is illustrated by what happened next: 'Tester and I buried the hatchet ere long, and became friends. He was a sportsman, and made a book on p.p [point-to-point] races; I often had a bet with him; and I recall that when Butterfly won the Oaks he paid me £6.'

Despite this aptitude for gaining weight, which he proved in later life to have in abundance, in his youth his slender figure precluded selection for the Blues in his first two years. He did make the Brasenose Torpid in his first term and then the College's first eight for his first summer. Throughout his bump-racing career, he only ever only suffered one bump – in that first Torpid, when another rower's oar broke, enabling Exeter to go Head. Even as he gained weight, strength and reputation, however, Brasenose did not quite go Head of the River during his undergraduate days. Shortly afterwards, though, he was back for two of the glorious hat-trick years of 1865–7. In 1865 and 1867, Woodgate stepped into the boat. In 1865, Brasenose went Head of the River and there was quite a night in College. Woodgate was impressed with the Vice-Principal of the College, Dr Menzies, who helped to his rooms the No 7 who 'had thoroughly saturated himself with toasts' and was swearing profusely, and then, when the student came to apologise the next morning. 'The Vice cut him short. "Shake hands, Mr I. We don't go Head of the River every day".'

Brasenose did, however, retain the headship for the following two summers. In 1866, Woodgate was busy preparing a Kingston crew for Henley when Robert Bridges (later the Poet Laureate) stroked Corpus to bump Brasenose, but BNC regained the headship and held it. Woodgate had made it back for the finale and approved not only of Brasenose winning but of Corpus' graciousness: 'Corpus behaved so nicely, and were so sportingly warm in their congratulations to BNC on the unique coup, that an instant especial entente cordiale was inaugurated between the two crews; and for long afterwards no bump supper of either college was complete without the attendance of the whole crew of the other.'

In 1867, Bridges and Woodgate were the coaches but 'F Crowder of BNC (afterwards MFH [Master of Fox Hounds]), who had rowed 6 for Oxford at Easter, got seedy; and I had to take his seat at scratch, to hold the headship.' On one night, as Brasenose 'went down last to the stations, with all the confident swagger of a head boat', the 'No 7's [R F Rumsey's] oar snapped like a carrot', just as the five-minute gun sounded. Woodgate had a friend on the bank, Bullock, the Lincoln captain, who was coaching rather than rowing, and who sprang into action: a replacement oar was fetched with seconds to spare and Brasenose duly held off Corpus to go Head of the River. The celebrations, as can be imagined, were as if the whole College, accompanied by the Corpus and Lincoln crews, was repeating the excesses of his Lady Barbara night in hall.

Christopher Dodd tells the story, somewhat at a tangent to his main task, in *The Oxford & Cambridge Boat Race* (1983):

Sometimes life has been stranger than fiction, in the bumps as elsewhere. In 1867 the Head crew Brasenose faced a crisis on the last day. Their head coach 'Guts' Woodgate had to get into the boat at the last minute because one man was seedy. Corpus, coached by the poet Robert Bridges, gave them a run night after night. On one of them Brasenose were in the Gut moving downstream to the start when Rumsey's oar snapped like a carrot just as the five-minute gun went off. The captain of Lincoln, who was on the bank as a coach, immediately sent sprinters to the barges on behalf of BNC while Woodgate's men got on the start. Woodgate hailed another friend who was in a gig with ladies and borrowed the best stick on board to make up the full complement of weapons; but it was of little use, he said, beyond that of a lady's fan. Bow took the fan, the second gun fired and they waited for the worst. Then Bullock raised a shout and the Brasenose men saw their spare oar coming down the bank at twenty miles an hour. They got it twenty-five seconds before the starting gun, and kept the headship. There was an almighty big drink in the college afterwards, with the Corpus and Lincoln eights as guests.

The rival coach, Robert Bridges, who stroked Corpus as an undergraduate and the Old Etonians at the Paris Regatta, was the man who later brought Gerard Manley Hopkins' poetry to public attention, and then himself became Poet Laureate. Woodgate introduces his discussion of that 1867 saga by explaining that,

> I was up for the summer term to coach BNC, not meaning to row; but as often as not I coached Corpus, while Bridges instructed my men. (Coaches each learn a lot, by swapping pupils like this; otherwise they have a tendency to run into a groove, and to get blind to one fault while laying siege to another.)

Just as Woodgate admired Warden Sewell, he was full of praise for the Principal of Brasenose, Dr Craddock, known as 'The Chief', for supporting the sportsmen of the College wholeheartedly, without presuming to dictate how they should go about their sport or their celebrating.

Woodgate hardly mentions his studies in this massive memoir, despite three substantial chapters on Oxford. Most accounts are silent on his scholarly achievements. One record of the Blues, however, records his honours in 1863 in the Final Honours School as Fourth Class. Cook in *The Field* gave credit for his earlier reputation:

> His spirit and energy were as inexhaustible as his classical quotations, for he had been a ripe and good scholar in his youth, with an astonishing memory for Aeschylus and Homer, which he could reel off by the yard.

In Greats, however, facility with the classical languages is not enough for Schools.

Of all his rowing successes, *The Field* chose to accompany news of his death with a photograph of the Kingston Rowing Club. Another famous rower, and Vincent's member, Frank Willan, wrote to explain the context of the image:

> The photograph of the Kingston Rowing Club eight which won the Grand Challenge Cup at Henley Regatta in 1865, is interesting from the fact that it shows my dear old friend, the late W B Woodgate, at a time when he was a very handsome man and just about in his prime as a finished oarsman. It is taken just outside the old boat-house at Henley, where at that time all the racing boats were housed … I had left Eton the

previous year, having rowed in the Eton crew which won the Ladies' Plate for the first time in 1864, but I had not yet matriculated at Oxford. My dear old friend, who was captain of the crew and also, I think, captain of the Kingston rowing club, enlisted me (I suppose as a promising youngster) to row in this crew. The final heat was rowed against a light but fast London Rowing Club eight, in a heavy storm of rain, and won by two-and-a-half lengths in 7' 25". I believe that, at that date, this was record time, and not bad over the old course on fixed seat and from the outside station. The Rev R W Risley, who rowed stroke, was a fine oar and splendidly backed up by Woodgate at seven.

Risley was one of the heroes ahead of Woodgate at Radley. Later in the 1860s, Frank Willan had been in the Oxford four which beat Harvard in a race that ensured the popularity of rowing in the United States. In 1920, he was out on the water with Woodgate only months before the latter's death. Sir Theodore A Cook, editor of *The Field*, paints the picture of Woodgate in the summer of 1920:

> Few expected his death who saw him in the terrible weather of last Henley, where he was taking out ladies, as was his invariable custom, in company with a niece of whom he was particularly proud; and when he sculled several miles with Frank Willan, I believe, just to show what the old'uns could do if they liked.

Woodgate's personal experience of the water at Henley thus spanned the late 1850s and the start of the 1920s. Born in 1840, he knew Thomas Staniforth, the stroke of Oxford's winning crew in the first Boat Race, held at Henley in 1829, and met all the survivors of both crews, as of the 'glorious seven', the victorious 1843 Oxford crew who had to row one short.

Like many members of the Club he founded, W B Woodgate was not only good at his sport and an inspiration to others, he also helped raise standards through coaching and writing. Twenty years after his own triumphs in the Boat Race, Woodgate was coaching both Oxford and Cambridge. In the letter quoted earlier in this chapter, Fairbairn records the impact Woodgate made:

> I shall never forget his coming to coach the Cambridge crew at Ely in 1883. Not only did he pick the crew and seat us as we were to race, but the variety of topics

in which he showed a deep knowledge was extraordinary. First he was writing a sermon to be preached the next Sunday; then he settled the crew; then he got into a discussion with myself as to the best grasses for Australia; then he gave us good advice as what not to do after training, explaining the different condition a horse should be in to race in the Derby and to go to the stud.

Woodgate's version focuses more on the rowing and the quality of the Boat Race:

I coached both crews an equal number of days, and one day took Cambridge on a morning tideway course, and caught the train to Taplow in time for Oxford's afternoon show. Of course one is glad to see one's own colour win, where it merits victory: but the chief sentiment that grows upon us is a desire to see the standard of UBC oarsmanship maintained high. It is small satisfaction to see Oxford win with a bad crew, beating a still-worse Cantab team. Far more satisfactory to see a tiptop crew win, even though it be from the rival club.

Woodgate was also known for challenging authority. In particular, he caused the Stewards at Henley to clarify their rules on more than one occasion. Irritated by the difficulty of competing in so many events when the schedule was designed with the interests of spectators rather than rowers in mind, he eventually drew up a revised programme, which was accepted. Along the way, he tried competing in more than one pair in the Silver Goblets of 1866, using an assumed name, Wat Bradgate, which he also deployed as an author of fiction, with M M Brown, and under his own name with E L Corrie. Woodgate and Corrie won. Corrie and Brown won the following year but in between times the Stewards ruled that competitors could only enter under their own names.

More famously, he challenged the authorities over their insistence that fours should carry a cox. Here he both won and lost the battle before decisively winning the war. The idea had come from a Canadian crew in the Paris Regatta. On his only trip to a foreign country, Woodgate not only won his own race but became excited at this innovation and determined to bring a Brasenose four to the next Henley without a cox. A smaller boat was therefore possible and duly built. Woodgate gave notice of his intention. Another Vincent's member, and good friend of Woodgate, W Wightman Wood, objected on behalf of University College. The Stewards ruled that the boats must start with a cox. Woodgate loved to quibble with such edicts, interpreting the words literally, in order to deflate the pomposity of the establishment. He determined that the boat would start with a cox but that the cox would then jump overboard. This is what happened but there were problems. The boat did not have space for a cox. That was the point. So the cox had to perch precariously. Then the chosen cox, Fred Weatherly, could not swim, so nearly drowned. Woodgate did not have much time for coxes, however, and was more interested in winning. The Brasenose crew were delayed at the start, given the need to avoid Weatherly while others saved his life. The boat went on to finish first but was then disqualified. Soon afterwards, however, the Stewards acknowledged that there should be coxless fours and authorised the change that Woodgate had, in this country pioneered.

Sir Theodore Cook gives a positive account of this classic Woodgate episode:

> Apart from his actual victories, the most characteristic episode of his racing days there was his sending the Brasenose cox overboard at the start of the Stewards' and steering his four with his feet. ... They were disqualified for passing the post without a coxswain, and we can still imagine the Boanergic elegance with which Woodgate argued his case against the authorities for days – and years – afterwards. In 1873, when the race was made coxswainless, he won his moral victory. Nothing but defeating a railway company in an action at law [could] have given him so much pleasure.

In the interests of balance, however, it is worth retrieving Fred Weatherly's view of this incident from his autobiography, *Piano & Gown*, in 1926. Woodgate does not emerge quite so well from the cox's version. Weatherly tells us that his godfather was Thompson from that heroic Oxford crew of the seven who beat Cambridge eight in 1843 (when they were not allowed to replace Fletcher-Menzies who had fainted). Weatherly was an undergraduate at Brasenose. He went on to a more successful career than Woodgate at the Bar, eventually becoming King's Counsel, and has achieved his own immortality as the composer of the lyrics of 'Danny Boy'. As Vincent's, of which he was not a member, celebrates its 150th anniversary, this song reaches its centenary. He paints a sadder picture of being the cox of the coxless four in which Woodgate, at two in the boat, 'did the steering via a pedal and wire attached to the rudder'. Weatherly explains that,

I had already steered my College boat at Oxford, but in 1868 I made my first appearance at Henley – which I hoped might lead to the higher honour of steering the 'Varsity Eight. The crew was in training at Henley under W B Woodgate, who was then an acknowledged oarsman of great skill and with a command of picturesque, not to say violent, language. It always struck me as strange that strong-tongued though he was on the river-bank, in court he was the mildest-mannered man that ever addressed judge and jury ... Two days before the race the stewards passed a special rule: No boat shall start without a cox. That could be evaded by taking a cox to the start and dropping him after the word 'go'. And accordingly I was wired for. I did not know for what I was wanted. I knew our boat was at Henley, and the telegram came from Henley and was signed 'Woodgate'. And no one ever started to take up the post of Viceroy of India with greater pride and speculation than I did ... The result of the race was announced in the Standard the next morning as follows. Henley: The Ladies' Plate: Brasenose won by eight lengths, but was disqualified for having thrown their cox overboard! This was the first tidings my mother received about me since I had left home, and I believe her sobbing remark was: 'disqualified indeed ..., they ought to be tried for attempting to murder the poor dear boy' ...Woodgate died some years ago, the same quaintly dressed old bird to the last.

As far as rowing is concerned, Cook deserves the last word, which is really an admission that there never could be a last word when Woodgate and rowing were concerned:

I could fill columns more (as he could have done himself) about his rowing; for, as the historian of the Boat Race has said, 'he has probably rowed and won more races, done more coaching, seen more, said more, and written more of and about University and College rowing than any other two of his contemporaries put together'. If I were asked to single out one point (among so many!) in which he was pre-eminent all his life, it would be his amazing judge of pace, in which I have never known his equal, either in estimating the speed of a crew or in judging the excellence of a boat, or in giving pontifical decisions about tide and stream. We shall all know far more about the Styx than ever Virgil or Dante dreamed, now Woodgate will meet us on that shadowy towpath.

But how did Woodgate make a living? There were two main channels, the law and journalism. *The Times* reported that Woodgate,

> was called to the Bar in 1872, when he joined the Oxford Circuit. He came from the University to the Inner Temple as a student with a remarkable record in athletics. At the Bar he practised largely in the Central Criminal Court and at the North London Sessions. At one period he waged war on the railway companies. Acting according to his view of the strict letter of the law, he insisted that a railway ticket was the only evidence of a passenger's contract with the railway co[mpany], and he therefore declined to surrender his ticket until the full journey had been made. The record of one of his actions against a railway co[mpany] is preserved in the Law Reports. He took a return first-class ticket one Christmas Eve from Paddington to Bridgnorth, a station on the branch line of the Great Western Company, intending to travel by a train which was advertised to run through. The weather was foggy. There were crowded carriages and there had been a collision on the main line. The train in which Mr Woodgate was travelling started late, and it was delayed by the fog and the excessive traffic. He missed the train on the branch line, and was detained at the junction, where there was little accommodation. The company refused a special train, and in the end Mr Woodgate travelled, at his own request, in a carriage attached to a goods train. The journey took 10 hours, instead of six as advertised. In a County Court action Mr Woodgate was awarded £1 damages, but the judgment was reversed on appeal, the Court holding that the conditions of the time bills, which were referred to on the back of the ticket, were incorporated in the contract, and that there was no evidence of wilful misconduct by the company.

Woodgate's own account of this is slightly but significantly different. He knew the opposing counsel and the judges well: 'It was Hawkins and A L Smith, two of the best friends that I had on the Bench, who formed the Divisional Court that decided Woodgate v Great Western Railway.' And guess who was counsel against him? 'My old "aquatic blue" friend, Wightman Wood, now County Court Judge, was for the railway'. Wood was the person who had objected to the coxless four innovation and sought the Stewards' ruling. He had also been a president of Vincent's. He asked Woodgate,

Would I, as a sportsman, consent to give the GWR a run for its life, and agree to a statement of case for appeal, which would leave open the issue whether or not their muteness as to the Slough block was enough to amount to wilful misconduct … To oblige, I assented; case was stated, and Hawkins and Smith ruled against me, that I just fell short of direct evidence of the necessary wilful phase of misconduct … The GWR had previously agreed to bear all the costs of appeal, both sides – if I made the sporting concession asked for as to statement of case. So I lost my thirty shillings damages; but the winners stood a sumptuous dinner at the Whitehall Club, to bury the hatchet (if any) of nominal legal conflict; and I think I managed to take on board quite my valuation of abandoned damages in good liquor. And the GWR and I have been the best of friends ever since.

The Times said a pound, Woodgate said thirty shillings (£1.50). The judges and opposing counsel also remained on good terms with Woodgate. A L Smith, a Cambridge rowing Blue and later a Lord Justice and Master of the Rolls 'was always game to bet me a new hat on the Boat Race … even when public favour and market odds might seem to be dead against the hopes of his own club'.

The Times regarded him as a great personality and sportsman, rather than a great lawyer, but one who contributed to the law's reputation:

By the death of Mr Woodgate a picturesque personality passes from the precincts of the Temple. The days have gone when he might have had rivals in the characters whom Charles Lamb met in King's Bench Walk. He was the last of an old, vigorous, and 'tut-tut' style of lawyer, sportsman, and gentleman. When he walked through the Courts and lanes as he would do sometimes with a low-crowned top hat, an Inverness cape, and knee-breeches with box-cloth leggings, his was a conspicuous and a welcome figure. His appearance was an anachronism, which was full of dignity nevertheless, and it made those who saw the man live momentarily in the past – in a period when the law and sport were really great. It is true that he was not a great lawyer, but men who are not great lawyers are often the most human and typical representatives of the law. He certainly was a great sportsman and a lover of the best form of country life … He was also the founder of Vincent's at Oxford, to become a mere member of which seems glory enough to many an undergraduate.

Woodgate's rowing journalism was first class, as were his rowing textbooks: *Oars and Sculls, and how to use them* (1874), *Boating* (1888), *Rowing and Sculling Illustrated* (1889). He was not only a writer of columns on rowing and of leaders but a pioneering force behind four magazines: *Vanity Fair, Land and Water*, the *Pall Mall Gazette* and *The Field*.

He enjoyed in his journalism ranging beyond the quality of the rowing itself to encompass bad form on the river-bank and good sportsmanship on the water. For *Vanity Fair*, for instance, he lambasted those whose fashion sense he faulted (although he was a fine one to judge), berating 'land-lubbers' for wearing blazers of tennis and cricket clubs that were brightly coloured 'Joseph coats' and 'monstrosities'. He praised sportsmanship, as when, in 1893: 'Guy Nickalls had an easy win in the Sculls. Everyone appreciated the sportsmanlike manner in which he pulled up for a restart with Boyd, the Dublin sculler, when the latter had jammed his slide and stopped for repairs.' He defended good sportsmen from accusations of bad sportsmanship: 'The outcry against Thames for boring the Frenchmen in their heat was only excusable under the impulse of chivalry to visitors. No sane man who has seen Thames R.C.'s performances year after year ought to have dreamed of supposing that a bit of bad steering inferred foul play. The T.R.C. are too thorough sportsmen for any such game. Anyone may make an error in the heat of a race.'

Woodgate's status as a character arose from more than all this. As *The Times* observed,

> One of the last of the Bohemians, whose personality will be missed by circles of friends wide as were his own interests, at the Bar, in social life, and in many fields of sports, has been removed by the death, which occurred at Southampton yesterday, of Mr Walter Bradford Woodgate, in his 81st year.

The Times enjoyed the breadth of Woodgate's interests. Citing his own account, noting that, according to his *Reminiscences*,

> [Woodgate] had a share in the making of the steeplechase rules; he played a not unimportant part in explaining the meaning of the search for Livingstone by the Royal Geographical Society; his book suggests that he inspired Pasteur in his hydrophobia

discovery, and one chapter is devoted to the first true and authentic account of the parentage of James I. Among other works from his pen were the Badminton Library book on 'Boating', a novel or two, and 'A Modern Layman's Faith'.

The Field enjoyed his status as a 'character':

> We are in no way disparaging our good old friend and valued contributor when we say that he was what men of the last generation would have called a 'character', by which we mean that he took his own line, and was not inclined to rule his life, or his attire, by the ordinary fashion of the day … It was perhaps partly to this disregard of what many would call les convenances, partly to the fact that he combined other work with that of the Bar, partly to a strong conviction of the justice and accuracy of his own opinions, and consequent intolerance of those of others, that he fell short of brilliant professional success. Unquestionably, he was a man of great ability and vast information. There was hardly a subject that could be mentioned on which he had not something, generally much, to say … he was a man of the utmost kindliness of heart. He would take the greatest trouble, would put himself to the utmost inconvenience, to help any of his friends …

If we had to take one lesson for students in this century from Woodgate the Sportsman and one from Woodgate the Bohemian, the former would be that even the greatest oarsman of the 19th century did not win a Blue in the first half of his undergraduate studies. He had to work at his weight and strength. But his memory lives on not only through his legendary reputation in rowing but through having the 'guts' to set up something as an undergraduate, steer it and coach it a bit on occasional trips back to Oxford but ultimately to entrust it to successive generations to make something of it. As for the Bohemian, Woodgate summed up his personal creed in three words, 'Sport, sympathy, sincerity', meaning that he valued beyond measure the friendships of characters who shared these values: 'Life has, of itself, been worth living, if only to have held such of these by the hand and shared their salt.' This is why he founded Vincent's in 1863 and why it flourishes 150 years later.

CHAPTER 2

1863–1913: The Pioneers

In the decade after Vincent's opened in 1863, half a dozen Club members were in the Oxford University team that won the FA Cup. That is all the more astonishing because neither the Cup nor the Football Association existed when Vincent's was founded.

To appreciate such an era as Vincent's opening years, the story of Oxford becoming the only university ever to win the FA Cup is one of three preliminary points that together set the scene. First, the dates of some other illustrious sporting foundations show this was a pioneering era in sport. Second, that in turn indicates the scale of success of pioneering Vincent's men through that team performance in winning the FA Cup. Third, the diversity of the characters and their individual successes will be illustrated by one of that team and a couple of other members from Vincent's first decade. These sketches set the context in which this chapter can then gallop from Woodgate's 'originals' through a few sample members and presidents of successive decades from the Club's foundation to the threshold of the Great War.

The Football Association was only founded later in the same year that Vincent's opened, 1863. In 1871 came the Rugby Football Union and in 1873 the Scottish Football Union, soon renamed as the Scottish Rugby Union. In 1880, the Amateur Athletic Association and the Amateur Boxing Association were founded, followed by the Amateur Rowing Association in 1882 and then the Amateur Swimming Association and Amateur Hockey Association in 1886. Before W B Woodgate founded Vincent's, only in cricket, through the private members' club of the MCC having been established in 1787 and issuing the first Laws in 1788, was there what today would be recognised as a national governing body of a major sport played by students.

On the pitch, the FA Cup did not begin until the 1871–72 season. What became the Oxford University Association Football Club was formed by students in November 1871. Oxford entered the Cup competition in the 1872–73 season, beating Crystal Palace in their first game, played at Kennington Oval. By Boat Race day in 1873, the Oxford University team had reached the FA Cup Final at their first attempt, with a couple of Vincent's members in the side, F H Birley and R W S Vidal (who had played for Wanderers when they won the first Cup Final). Playing at Lillie Bridge in London in the morning, to allow time to watch the rowers in the afternoon, Oxford lost 2-0 to Wanderers.

Birley was one of the first footballers to play for England. He also went on to win the Cup twice as captain of Wanderers. He played county cricket for Lancashire before his footballing successes and for Surrey afterwards. He competed in varsity athletics, throwing the hammer. As this combination suggests, he was a champion at the then popular challenge of throwing the cricket ball. He became a barrister. Vidal had played for Wanderers when they won the first Cup Final and when he was still a schoolboy at Westminster. He won a rugby Blue in 1872 and was the first president of the Oxford University Golf Club. He set up the only goal in the first Cup Final and was one of the first players to be known as 'the prince of dribblers'. He became a clergyman in later life.

In 1874, Oxford reached the final again, this time at the Oval against Royal Engineers and with a majority of the team being members of Vincent's. Birley and Vidal were joined by R H Benson, A H Johnson, C E Nepean and W S Rawson. Benson was a noted forward (a patron of the arts, a miler and president of Oxford University Athletics Club) and Rawson was reported to be the best half-back in the country, but Nepean made the difference, having been unavailable the previous year when selected and now playing in goal, although he was also an accomplished forward. This game made it a hat-trick of Cup Final appearances by Vidal. Oxford won 2-0. Shortly afterwards, Oxford played their first varsity football match against Cambridge, also at the Oval, winning 1-0. Oxford played in two more FA Cup Finals, losing in 1877 and 1880, before bowing out of the competition, more because players were also in demand from their old public schools than simply because professional sides were emerging, but the University had more than played its pioneering part in attracting attention to what has become the most popular team sport in the world. Oxford remains the only university side to have won the FA Cup or indeed to have played in any FA Cup Finals. Given Wembley's delightful practice of putting up the names of the teams and the year when they first won the Cup, there is an annual reminder of this achievement.

Five of the Vincent's members among that FA Cup-winning team were current students but A H Johnson, then of Exeter, had become a member of Vincent's in 1867, that is to say before the sport of football as we know it had been formalised, and was chaplain and Fellow of All Souls by the time he won the FA Cup in 1874. He had already taught at several colleges and continued to be a tutor for many. An historian, towards the end of Vincent's first half-century he was so distinguished that he was invited to give the prestigious Ford Lectures in 1909.

Even his worst enemy, J C Masterman, a later Vincent's member, conceded that Johnson's lecture series, published as a book under the title *History of the Small Landowner* was a 'minor classic', while Masterman (of whom more anon in the next chapter) damns with the faint praise of being 'textbooks' Johnson's *Europe in the 16th Century*, 'a model textbook', and *The Age of the Enlightened Despot*, a 'long-lived textbook' for which Johnson was 'probably most widely known'. Even if a couple of them were textbooks, Johnson's titles are not the kind associated with books by most FA Cup winners.

Arthur was married to Bertha who became the founding principal of what is now St Anne's. The couple were pioneers of what is today called widening participation. In the same decade as winning the FA Cup, Arthur Johnson gave the first of the 'Lectures for Ladies' in Oxford and the first lecture of the Oxford Extension Movement, speaking at King Edward's School, Birmingham. Vera Brittain writes of the former, in *The Women at Oxford*, that: 'When the Rev. Arthur Johnson gave the first lecture the audience overflowed the room; another had to be used, and the success of the series was guaranteed.' The latter gives Johnson a claim to be a founding father of the movement which is now identified with Kellogg College. In other words, he was one of the best footballers of his time, a serious scholar and a pioneer of widening participation. Whatever else motivated his election to Vincent's, it could not have been his outstanding achievements for Oxford in football because they not only came later, but could not even have been imagined in Vincent's first decade. A H Johnson was by no means Vincent's only pioneering scholar-athlete.

The pioneering nature of Vincent's in sport and politics can be illustrated by another 'ordinary' member from its first decade, the Earl of Rosebery, who joined the Club in the Lent term of 1869. His college, Christ Church, had not provided any of the original members in 1863 because, Woodgate tells us, the House was so well supplied with clubs of its own. Like Woodgate, Rosebery was fond of horse-racing. Unlike Woodgate, he became Prime Minister in 1894, having already served as Foreign Secretary and had masterminded Gladstone's famous Midlothian campaign, which pioneered modern electioneering. Lord Rosebery is not the only Oxford-educated Prime Minister to have left the University without a degree (he wrote about another in his biography of the Earl Chatham, William Pitt the Elder, who left Trinity College due to illness), but he is the only one to have left after a disagreement with the authorities over his refusal to give up owning a racehorse.

Lord Rosebery owned horses which won all the classic races. In particular, three of his horses won the Derby – Ladas in 1894, Sir Visto in 1895 and Cicero in 1905. The first two victories were remarkable for another reason, beyond being in successive years. Although he was only Prime Minister for some fifteen months, his short term of office included those Derby days in 1894 and 1895 when his horses won. What a double! Just as he refused to give up owning racehorses at Oxford, he is said to have told a Downing Street official that, 'Politics and racing are inconsistent, which is a good reason to give up politics'. At the beginning of the 20th century, it was Rosebery who led the trustees of the Rhodes Scholarships which have brought so many scholar-athletes of distinction to Oxford. He was nominated as a trustee by Cecil Rhodes himself who was also a member of Vincent's and who had gone into business with other Vincent's members.

It is not the case, however, that Vincent's men were all cup winners, dons at All Souls or Prime Ministers. To put the Club in perspective, it is worth acknowledging from the outset that eccentric characters could find a place from this first decade, with Vincent's including the occasional member who had no particular interest in, or talent for, any sport. Moreover, you can never tell where a Vincent's member will pop up in life or, of course, what unconnected 'events' (to use a word associated with a Vincent's Prime Minister, Harold Macmillan) will bring a relatively obscure Vincent's man to attention a century or more after his death. For example, in Vincent's history, 2013 is significant for the Club's 150th anniversary. In the wider world, a surprising feature of the year has been the first papal resignation for some 700 years. A 'sede vacante', or vacant see (of Rome), has for all those centuries only arisen on the death of a Pope, but when Benedict XVI resigned on grounds of old age and ill health, church historians could turn to a rare book by an authoritative insider on *Sede*

Vacante, written by a Vincent's man. Woodgate wrote about this fellow Brasenose student that, 'Grissell was a non-athlete, but quiet and refined and popular; later he changed his creed for that of Rome, and became a chamberlain to the Pope'. (Woodgate is not in this tale really focused on Grissell but is recounting that Bobby Shepherd, who rowed with him at Oxford and Henley, and Grissell were two of his Brasenose contemporaries who stuttered.)

For much of this first half-century of Vincent's, Grissell was one of the most senior officials in the Vatican, a remarkable post for an Englishman who was still an Anglican when he joined Vincent's in 1863. Hartwell de la Garde Grissell, educated first at Harrow in the 1850s, became a convert to Catholicism in 1868 (received into the Church by Woodgate's godfather, Henry Manning, by then the Archbishop of Westminster) and in 1869 a Chamberlain of Honour to Pope Pius IX. This was a lively period in Rome, with the First Vatican Council opening on 8 December, the Feast of the Immaculate Conception, 1869, declaring the dogma of papal infallibility in 1870 and then being suspended when Italy, during the Franco-Prussian War, annexed the Vatican.

These senior posts lapse with the death (or resignation) of a Pope, but Grissell was reappointed to serve in the same capacity by Pope Leo XIII in 1878 and, after his long reign, again by Pope Pius X in 1903. Leo XIII was greatly influenced by Cardinal Manning in expounding what is now known as Catholic Social Teaching and which is credited with underpinning modern political thought about the common good and such notions as subsidiarity. Leo was impressed with the longevity and resilience of Queen Victoria, the two exchanging greetings and presents on their various jubilees, and was interested in Grissell's accounts of Oxford life. When not in Rome, Grissell continued until his death in 1907 to live in Oxford by Vincent's at 60 High Street and championed the cause of Catholic students who, largely through his efforts in persuading Leo XIII, became free to attend the University, which was not the Church's position when Vincent's began. Grissell might well have drawn on his experience of Vincent's, because he used his Oxford property in much the same manner to provide social space for Catholic students. Grissell is therefore reckoned to be the founder of university Newman Societies, Catholic associations which could be seen as modelled on Vincent's. Grissell was working in Rome when the consistories were held in which two of Oxford's sons, Manning and Newman, became cardinals.

In his book *Sede Vacante*, Grissell gives his impressions of the context of what became a very long and remarkable Conclave, with the Austro-Hungarian Emperor purporting to apply a veto on the cardinal who was leading the early rounds of ballots. There is a Vincent's dimension to the grand conclusion of this Conclave as Grissell describes the scene on Sunday, 9 August 1903, when he was waiting on the new Pope, Pius X, on the day of his coronation:

The Holy Father shortly before 8.30 came out of his private apartment, and I at once hastened forward to meet him, and having knelt and kissed his hand, asked him for his blessing for myself and our congregation at St. Aloysius', Oxford, which he graciously granted. I told him that I felt sure it would interest His Holiness to know that today, the 9th of August, his own Coronation day, was also that of my own King, Edward VII, and that on this very day a year ago, in the Abbey of Westminster, I had the honour of being on duty, and in the service of my own Sovereign, as Gold Staff Officer. This seemed to greatly interest him, and I can boast that probably I am the only man in the world who has had this unique honour of serving both his temporal and his spiritual Sovereigns on the occasion of their Coronations, on the very same day two years in succession.

That was indeed an unlikely double, but so was the fact that Edward VII and Hartwell de la Garde Grissell were both members of Vincent's.

In the year of Grissell's death, 1907, William Theodore Heard of Balliol, a member of Vincent's, won his rowing Blue alongside other Vincent's members who went on to win Olympic gold medals. Fifty years later, William Heard became a cardinal, elevated by Pope John XXIII, who called the Second Vatican Council. Heard is often described as the first Scottish cardinal, or the first Scottish cardinal since the Reformation, although his work was in England and mostly in Rome, ultimately as the leading judge of the Church's marriage tribunal. Cardinal Heard participated in the Second Vatican Council and in the conclave that elected Pope Paul VI in 1963.

So Vincent's can number a cardinal with a rowing Blue as well as the non-sporting confidante of a 'red' Pope among its alumni. As with the All Souls don and the Prime Minister, it is difficult to say what influence Vincent's had on their development, as opposed to the impact of their colleges or tutors or subjects or peers or schools or other societies or sporting experiences. Even if the relationship was fraught, as with Christ Church and Lord Rosebery, it can be healed over time and might have been influential in provoking a Vincent's member into achievement, almost to spite, or at least in spite of, the authorities. It is possible that those who had known Rosebery at school might have anticipated him becoming Prime Minister or owning Derby winners, but when they joined Vincent's it would have been miraculous if anyone had anticipated Johnson winning a cup that did not exist or Grissell, then an Anglican, becoming within that first decade a senior aide to the Pope.

These three illustrations of colourful characters with a hinterland that is more than sporting are consistent with the official *History of the University of Oxford, Vol VI: Nineteenth Century Oxford* (1997) which summarises how Vincent's swiftly developed its reputation:

> The most important mark of athletic status was, of course, the blue; and sporting prestige was institutionalized in Vincent's Club, founded in 1863, which rapidly became 'the premier Social Club of the University'. Its membership was restricted to one hundred, and its rules made it relatively easy to blackball candidates for election. At its foundation it was composed principally of the friends of the founder, the oarsman W B Woodgate of Brasenose, and it held a particular attraction for men from the nearby colleges (notably Brasenose, University College, and Merton) who resented the inconvenient walk to the Union. Only slowly did it acquire its modern character as the club for blues – indeed, not until the 1870s do we see the emergence of the concept of 'the blue' in a recognizably modern sense – though already by the 1880s very few non-blues held office in the club. In 1894 Isis could describe Vincent's as a 'sacred Temple … to those whom, by virtue of themselves, their athletic powers, and their social and general good-fellowship, a grateful University delighteth to honour'. Election to Vincent's had become 'the diploma which the University of Undergraduates grants in due season to her most successful and deserving sons'. (Isis no 59, 10 Nov 1894, 59–60) … At the height of its success, however, Vincent's was never straightforwardly a club for blues; in the 1890s they represented fewer than half of its members. The fact that Vincent's could claim pre-eminence over the Bullingdon (a club still dominated by the gentry and devoted to country sports) was an illustration of Oxford's changing values.

When Woodgate himself wrote about his 'originals', the first 40 he asked to become founding members of Vincent's, he explained that,

> In the official lists of Vincent's Club an error was made of recording as 'original members' all those whose subscriptions figure as paid in at the old Bank during the Lent term. Whoever compiled the list knew no better, and had nothing to guide him beyond the bank book; but as a matter of fact, a large number of the subscribers in Lent term, 1863, went through the ballot-box and joined us thus, a week or so after we opened. Many intimate friends, who had already sunk their term's subscription in the Union, hung back for the first week, thinking me over-sanguine and waiting for developments, but joined later.

Anyone writing about Vincent's 150 years or more later is bound to have considerable sympathy for the compiler of that list because that is how poor the record-keeping was in the beginning, and it deteriorated further before the recent Herculean efforts by the committee charged with preparing the Club for its anniversary.

Christ Church was so well supplied with clubs of its own that Woodgate could not persuade any of its members to join, but otherwise he was pleased with his 40, until the four from Magdalen resigned. This was because the originals were invited to a meeting on the first Sunday after opening to select the remaining new members but one veto ('black ball') in nine would debar a candidate and the very first person proposed, in alphabetical order, was another Magdalen man who was blackballed. The four Magdalen originals retaliated and, having a ninth of the votes, they blocked every other nominee.

So Woodgate names nine from Univ, seven from Merton, ten from BNC, two each from Pembroke, Balliol, Corpus and Exeter, plus one each from Trinity and Lincoln, as his first 36. Looking back just before the 50th anniversary, he was, 'proud to relate that of this pick of personal friends to support me in my new venture, a large majority historically have made their mark in the world, one way or another'. That seems to include three becoming Master of Fox Hounds, at least one becoming a leading Freemason and another becoming a 'popular man of society'.

In sporting terms, the three of the originals whose successes particularly impressed Woodgate were Jack Forster, F H Gooch and W H P Jenkins. Jack Forster, a president of Vincent's in 1865, beat Woodgate himself (the inaugural president in 1863) at Henley when winning Grand, Ladies' and Stewards' in a single day, as a 'wondrous stroke'. A Vincent's president in 1866, W H P Jenkins, went on to become Chairman of National Hunt. F H Gooch of Merton, who did not attain the presidency, became famous among students for his high-jumping exploits against Cambridge in the first varsity contest in athletics and around the town of Oxford. Woodgate revels in telling us of Gooch's more informal route to fame: 'A feat of Gooch's was to jump in and out of Merton Walk,' which used to

> run straight ... fenced both sides with iron spiked railings some 5ft 2ins in height. The path between them is, I believe, about 8ft wide. Gooch used to take the double fence 'in and out', landing on the path from Merton, and springing straight into the Corpus side of the garden. It must have wanted some nerve to do this.

Woodgate warns that a Magdalen man, known as 'Jumping Jones', attempting a similar challenge elsewhere, was badly spiked and insists that he does not intend to tempt anyone to their destruction but he does wonder 'whether any twentieth century Oxford talent [might] ever emulate these feats'.

It was on the river, naturally, that Woodgate had been goaded by friends in 1863 into turning into reality the intention he had often voiced of creating an alternative to the Union. He knew the printer, Vincent, who had rented out rooms above his shop on The High to the Union but who had fallen out with them over non-payment of rent. He locked them out, they broke in, he suggested they find other premises and they did. So for some years, 'Old Vincent', as Woodgate called him, started a 'reading-room' of his own, undercutting the Union, which charged a guinea a term, with his fee of 13s 6d. As it was convenient for Brasenose, Woodgate subscribed himself and was irked when numbers dwindled and Vincent closed the rooms in 1861. Woodgate blamed the Union and would not join that Society because it included 'certain of the blackest sheep who had been notoriously expelled with ignominy from public schools'. Others from Brasenose, University and Merton similarly shunned the Union.

So Woodgate negotiated with Vincent and was ready to open within four days of that challenge on the river by Hon C Ellis and C 'Sharks' Stanhope (sometimes known as Spencer-Stanhope), who both went on to become original members and presidents of Vincent's. When they hailed Woodgate and suggested they should meet at the Union, he declined in no uncertain terms. So they teased him, as Schools and the end of his undergraduate days approached, for not having provided the alternative to the Union that he was always promising. This was exactly how to secure Woodgate's attention and he knew just the setting and just the person in Vincent's and Old Vincent. It says much about Old Vincent and Woodgate that when the latter subscribed to the former's reading-rooms, they had met on the stairs one day and the former asked the latter whether he would like tickets to see Rarey, the horse-whisperer, perform. Of course he did.

In Vincent's folklore, then, the Club was at daggers drawn with the Union but in reality some students belonged to both, such as Nathaniel Curzon, later Viceroy of India, and other future politicians. Woodgate did, however, address his gripe with the Union – that they just let in anyone who was a member of the University, while making a pretence of selecting for good character – by fashioning his club as a more exclusive 'century' of members. Other aspects of Vincent's that have excited comment were the prohibitions on women and dogs, and the provision of free beer and postage. The first set of rules did not ban women. It was more that the University did not permit women to become members. Nor did the rules initially ban dogs although that was soon introduced. The free beer and postage were to avoid Proctors interfering with a commercial venture. There was one member of staff, John Brown, who combined the roles of 'steward, waiter, and petty cashier'. He was later supported and then succeeded by his son, who was unofficially known, inevitably, as Young John, and whose official title, 'High Steward', was thought to be too grand by Woodgate. The hospitality soon became legendary, as did the Club. Even in the 1860s, Woodgate had to thwart more than one attempt to increase the number of members allowed by the original constitution.

That first decade set the tone of the Club, which achieved immediate renown and which reflected the unconventional nature of the founder's character, so much so that it was full of people who disagreed with him, and he rather liked that. He could not get agreement on his preferred name, he could not get his originals all into his own club, the members eventually expanded beyond his magical figure of 100 and he could not keep his successors in those initial premises, there being four moves before the Club settled in its present home on the corner of King Edward Street and The High, above Shepherd & Woodward, in rooms leased from Oriel.

This is what fascinates many outside the Club who hear of Vincent's. There is a perception that sportsmen are rather unscholarly, unbalanced and deeply conservative. Yet a club for elite sportsmen at one of the most celebrated universities of all time was started by an unconventional undergraduate of eclectic interests and has flourished for 150 years, bringing together some of the most extraordinary characters, and doing much to promote sport both inside the University and beyond. When the call to arms came in the 20th century, the courage of the pioneering spirit was converted into heroism in two world wars. All through the first 100 years, the Club elected students who became sporting heroes. In the last 50 years, conventional wisdom has it that Oxbridge sport has spiralled downwards in quality and significance while graduates play for safety in focusing on their studies and then on 'safe' careers. The reality is that even in this latest phase, Vincent's members have achieved the highest honours in sport, in their studies, in jobs and in life.

Woodgate, writing as the 50th anniversary approached, had his own list of Vincent's members, beyond his originals, who had succeeded in the wider world. As he put it, 'a galaxy of future statesmen, divines and athletes, have adorned the club'. He singled out such lords as Jersey, Desborough, Rosebery and Randolph Churchill, then the Foreign Secretary Sir Edward Grey, various clerics and judges, Prince Christian Victor and an interesting juxtaposition in 'Cecil Rhodes (empire builder)' followed by 'C S Newton (oarsman, gentleman rider, and Jockey Club)'.

Attention can only be drawn here to a few stars from each decade.

At the start of the 1870s, J C Tinné was the president and at the end of the decade, the president was William Grenfell, later Lord Desborough. The former was the president of the OUBC when Harvard challenged Oxford to a boat race in 1868. Tinné accepted, other Vincent's members were in the coxed foursome and the comprehensive trans-Atlantic newspaper coverage of the race is credited with an outpouring of interest in rowing across the United States. This was truly a pioneering occasion, fraught with difficulties for Harvard who had to build and transport a boat before they could experience the course, but there was a boldness in accepting the challenge and in ensuring as fair a contest as possible. Cambridge were also challenged by Harvard but declined the opportunity. Tinné and his crew won.

By the end of the 1870s, the dominant figure in Oxford sport was William Grenfell of Balliol, who went on to run various sports, culminating in organising the London 1908 Olympics at short notice (when the eruption of Vesuvius prevented Italy from hosting the Games as intended) but to widespread acclaim, save in those same United States, who regarded the Olympics in London as biased against them. Before that, he had rowed in the dead-heat Boat Race in 1877, rowed again when Oxford won in 1878 and then been president of Oxford University Athletics Club in 1878 as well as president of Oxford University Boat Club and Vincent's in 1879. He had already served as secretary and treasurer of Vincent's. He enjoyed country sports and big game hunting. If Gooch liked jumping in and out of Merton, Grenfell liked challenges in the wider world. He swam the Niagara Falls, climbed the Matterhorn and rowed across the English Channel, all of which he accomplished as an early pioneer, and which would make quite a triathlon for any modern-day Vincent's member.

A quarter of a century after his rowing and athletics Blues, William Grenfell was still an active sportsman. He carried the flag and fenced in the 1906 Intercalated Games in Athens, when the short-lived idea was that in between the four yearly Olympics to be held around the world, there would be a mid-term Games in Athens. He was extremely active off the field of play as chair or president of the Amateur Athletic Association, Amateur Fencing Association, Amateur Swimming association, Amateur Wrestling Association and the MCC. He even has a claim to have been a pioneer in the West of Japanese martial arts, as president of the Bartitsu Club in London at the turn of the century, which later received some publicity when Arthur Conan Doyle described Sherlock Holmes as deploying 'Baritsu' techniques against Moriarty. He chaired many other non-sporting boards, was a Member of Parliament and later a member of the House of Lords and a Knight of the Garter. Above all, after dismal Games in Paris 1900 and St Louis 1904 had squandered the capital of the Olympic revival in Athens 1896, his magisterial organising of the 1908 London Games saved the Olympic movement and bolstered the standing in the world of what was then the United Kingdom of Great Britain and Ireland. If Woodgate was the W G Grace of rowing, Grenfell was the Seb Coe of 1908. As an undergraduate in the 1870s, William Grenfell rubbed shoulders in Vincent's with other pioneers of various sports.

In between these two towering presidents of the 1870s, a member of Vincent's who contributed greatly to the pioneering days of both football (in its various guises, handling and kicking) and athletics was Montague Shearman of St John's.

His book on both became the definitive work of instruction and history. Together with other Oxford sportsmen, Bernhard R Wise and Clement Jackson, he was responsible for founding the Amateur Athletic Association in the Randolph Hotel on 24 April 1880, whereupon one of Woodgate's chosen stars, the Earl of Jersey, became the first president. It is tempting to attribute many such developments in sport to Vincent's just because some or all of the people involved were connected to the Club. But Wise of Queen's, although president of the Oxford University Athletics Club, was more of a student politician, and it was his skills as president of the Oxford Union which contributed most to the diplomacy involved in bringing together the warring factions of athletics. He was later a relatively unsuccessful politician back home in his native Australia, finding it difficult to cope with voters and colleagues who resented his privileged education and accent. Jackson was a legend in days before athletic records were so clear-cut but is generally thought to have held the British and probably world record for the sprint hurdles. He famously retired from athletics after cutting his foot on an oyster shell in a hurdling race against W G Grace (who cut more of an athletic figure in those days). By the time of the AAA's foundation, he was a don at his old college, formally Magdalen Hall but by now known as Hertford. He only became an honorary member of Vincent's afterwards, in 1882. He was an inspirational figure as the most supportive of dons, serving as treasurer of OUAC for 60 years. All three founders, Jackson, Shearman and Wise, were scholars with First Class Honours and Wise won the University's Cobden Prize.

It would be fair to say that Shearman, as both a rugby player and an athlete, who also boxed and played lacrosse, epitomised the pioneering sporting all-rounders prized and fostered by Vincent's in the 1870s. Even in athletics, he was an all-rounder, a sprinter (100 yards in 10.2 seconds to win the varsity in 1876 and a shot-putter, 34 feet 9½ inches in 1879). The creation of the AAA in 1880 by Oxford men was a turning point in the history of athletics. Shearman became the honorary secretary, then vice-president, then president, as Vincent's first half century continued. Soon after starting the AAA he was called to the Bar; he took silk in 1903 and began Vincent's next 50 years as a High Court judge in 1914. He was one of 'three wise men' appointed to examine the causes of the 1916 Easter rebellion in Ireland. An old sporting injury caught up with him and he died in 1930. Like one of Vincent's FA Cup winners, Benson, Shearman was a patron of the arts.

The huge pioneering spirit of Vincent's in the 1870s can be glimpsed in two vignettes, of the most and least sporting of members. The Honourable Marshall Brooks of Woodgate's old college, Brasenose, a rugby Blue in 1873, set the world record for the high jump in the 1876 varsity match at Lillie Bridge, clearing 6 feet 2½ inches (1.89 metres). The magisterial history of Oxford University Athletics Club notes simply: 'It was not until 1887 that Brooks' world record was surpassed and as a 'Varsity match record, it stood for 72 years.' Frederick Webster is then quoted as the 'great athletics commentator':

> When jumping, Brooks ran straight at the bar and once told me before he died a few years ago, that although he could throw his feet up as high as he wanted, his main difficulty was getting his arms and particularly his elbows over the bar. He ran with his knees tucked up in front, took his body over with a forward jerk and landed on his toes. The late Sir Montague Shearman once told me that when Brooks first cleared 6ft, so great was the enthusiasm that the OUAC Hon Treasurer tossed his top hat in the air, but had to retrieve it sadly from a deep puddle on the old Marston Athletic Ground.

That treasurer was Vincent's Clement Jackson.

The highest leap in Oxford's philanthropy over the next 72 years, and still counting, came from another Vincent's member of the 1870s, Cecil Rhodes, who showed a pioneering spirit, not always to great acclaim, both in South African business and politics and in Oxford philanthropy. His studies at Oriel were in two spells, in between business concerns in South Africa. He was not a sportsman himself but appreciated those who were, and shared Woodgate's vision of the value of sport among all-round qualities. It could be said that he drew on Vincent's as the inspiration for his Rhodes Scholarships. As the 19th century came to an end, he received an honorary doctorate from Oxford. As the 20th began, his will provided for scholars to attend Oxford from the English-speaking world, with the addition of Germany once the Kaiser had insisted on English as a compulsory subject in German schools. Initially there were 52 each year, 32 from the USA with others from South Africa, what was then Rhodesia, parts of Canada, Australia, New Zealand, Bermuda and Jamaica. Rhodes envisaged that they would all be men but the trustees eventually allowed women. For many years, the four criteria for selection were:

1 'literary & scholastic attainments;
2 'energy to use one's talents to the full, as exemplified by fondness for and success in sports;
3 'truth, courage, devotion to duty, sympathy for and protection of the weak, kindliness, unselfishness and fellowship;
4 'moral force of character and instincts to lead, and to take an interest in one's fellow beings.'

Rhodes' will stated that 'no student shall be qualified or disqualified for election to a Scholarship on account of race or religious opinions'. The Rhodes Trust and the University go further in requiring now that selection for a Scholarship and admission to the University will be 'without regard to marital status, race, ethnic origin, colour, religion, sexual orientation, social background, or disability'.

If the first chair of the Rhodes Trustees was a Vincent's and former Prime Minister, Lord Rosebery, another Vincent's member, Sir Francis James Wylie, was one of the pivotal administrators of the scheme in its first half century. The current chair of the Rhodes Trustees, the former Vice-Chancellor of Oxford, Dr John Hood, is a Vincent's member, and one of Vincent's most senior and celebrated members, Dr Robin Fletcher, an Olympic medallist in hockey, is a former Warden of Rhodes House. Rhodes himself gave money directly to Vincent's and the Rhodes Trustees have in the past given to what Sir Anthony Kenny, another former Warden of Rhodes House, described as 'minor Oxford causes', including Vincent's. Many Rhodes Scholars are themselves members of Vincent's.

A phrase in Cecil Rhodes' will gave, as one of the original four criteria for the selection of a Scholar, 'his fondness of and success in manly outdoor sports such as cricket, football and the like'. Rhodes referred to this quality as 'brutality' when suggesting that it should count for about two-tenths of the decision, but it was put more elegantly (not only in correcting his 'of' to 'for') when it was presented by Selection Committees to prospective scholars as 'energy to use one's talents to the full, as exemplified by fondness for and success in sports'. Nowadays, candidates can illustrate the energy in other ways and there is no specific reference to sport. Nevertheless, Rhodes Scholars have over 100 years given Oxford a significant advantage over Cambridge in certain varsity contests, such as basketball, ice hockey, swimming and water polo. Some sporting Rhodes Scholars have not sought a Blue, concentrating instead on their studies or experimenting with sports other than their main one, or just not being allowed to play, for instance because they had played professionally in an era when the sports here were only open to amateurs, or because, given their future professional commitments in sport, the insurance would be prohibitive. In celebrating the 150th anniversary, some Vincent's members, including Rhodes Scholars, are contemplating establishing an awards scheme which brings home in a modest way to Vincent's the idea that Rhodes took, possibly from the Club itself, and applied on the grand scale.

In the 1880s, Vincent's presidents included A G G Asher in 1885, Ducker McLean in 1886 and H H Castens in 1887. A G G Asher was a Loretto schoolboy who went to Brasenose, gaining what we would now call Blues for rugby and athletics, as well as in cricket, where it already was called a Blue, played for Scotland, had his career ended by breaking a leg badly in a Scottish trial in 1887, became a lawyer and public servant, and president of the Scottish Rugby Union in 1929–30. A leading historian of Scottish rugby who 'saw a good deal of A G G Asher's football and cricket in Scotland, and … knew his 'form' on the track pretty well' considered that,

> The career of A G G Asher could only be done justice to in a much more extended and detailed treatment than I am in a position to attempt. As a triple 'Blue' at Oxford, A G G Asher won great honour for himself and renown for his school. In football he had the singular experience of acting as partner at quarter or half-back to A Rotherham in England and with R Don Wauchope in Scotland. Neither at the University nor in Scottish internationals have these partnerships ever been excelled or even equalled.

Rotherham, like Harry Vassall, was a Vincent's rugby player inducted recently into Twickenham's Hall of Fame. They are credited with pioneering more attacking and integrated play between forwards and backs. As Vincent's president at the time when the Oxford University Dramatic Society was being started, Asher was invited to become OUDS' first president, a sure sign that Vincent's had swiftly established itself as the leading club of men of action. OUDS shrewdly wanted to bridge any gulf between aesthetes and 'hearties' (sportsmen). Another Vincent's member of this era, Gilbert Bourne, father and grandfather of a remarkable rowing dynasty, bridged the gap beautifully between sport and art and between science and art in his own life and in his writing. Bourne was a rowing Blue in the 1880s, then one of several great Vincent's rowing coaches while a don at New College, and a writer about the sport when he was the Linacre Professor of Zoology. In his judgment, 'rowing is not a game' but an art, 'a gratification of an aesthetic sense of motion on the waters'.

It was not only in rugby that Asher was in illustrious company. Asher made his first-class debut for Oxford in the Parks against the MCC in 1883 (when another Vincent's man, Francis Pember, was playing for the opposition alongside E J C Studd, half-brother to Cambridge's famous cricketing and Christian missionary trio of Studds). In 1884, E J C Studd, listed as being of Abingdon, was elected to Vincent's as an honorary member. He played against Oxford in these games from 1883 to 1885, twice in 1884 and twice in 1885 – 110 and 44 for MCC v Oxford in 1885, 60 for Gentlemen. In 1886 Studd opened for MCC in a first-class game with W G Grace, who got a century and then took all ten Oxford wickets in their second innings – 10 for 49 off 36.2 (4 ball) overs.

F W Pember had become a member of Vincent's in Lent 1881, and his brother, H E Pember, was elected in Lent 1885. Each became secretary of the Club. Francis (or Frank) Pember had made it as far as the Freshmen's trial in 1881 and had played other games such as for the Perambulators against the Etceteras in the Parks, having the distinction of being run out in both innings. In this game, however, Pember was not out in each innings, including in the first his highest score in first-class cricket, 47. Pember became a barrister, then Warden of All Souls and Vice-Chancellor of Oxford. He used to amuse himself during boring meetings by translating English verse he knew off by heart into Latin or Greek. Stefan Collini in *Common Readings* tells us that the *Westminster Gazette* set a fortnightly competition in the 1890s and on to the First World War. It was 'most frequently won by F W Pember, the Warden of All Souls'. The All Souls historian A L Rowse wrote of his Warden, 'Not that Pember was an Empire man, he didn't care for the group inspired by Rhodes and Milner, the "Kindergarten". A Balliol friend of Grey and Asquith, he was a Little Englander'.

As for Asher's role as the pioneering president of OUDS, the first person to appear on stage in their first production, rather reluctantly reciting an uninspiring prologue written by Vincent's Lord Curzon, later Viceroy of India, was Vincent's

Cosmo Gordon Lang, later Archbishop of Canterbury. Although not a great sportsman himself, Lang encouraged muscular Christianity, especially football, when he was a young curate in Leeds. As Archbishop of Canterbury, Lang was one of three Vincent's men involved in the abdication crisis of 1936, the others being King Edward VIII himself, who became the Duke of Windsor (having been the Prince of Wales when a student at Magdalen), and his legal adviser, Sir (later Viscount) Walter Monckton.

The next president, D H 'Ducker' McLean, was from Australia. W B Woodgate argued at Henley that the regatta should be open to 'colonials', a term used then to refer to people from the Empire. Ducker McLean was a consummate oarsman and a successful rowing coach with a long Oxford winning streak. He died of trench fever while serving in the army in the Boer War in 1901, at the age of 37. A stylist of note, he was unluckily remembered primarily for one mishap as a rower, his first four Blues tending to be forgotten in favour of his fifth, when his oar broke and he was severely criticised (including by Woodgate) for not jumping in to lighten the boat. Not surprisingly, given the possibility of death in the polluted and cold Thames, with steamers also threatening anyone in the water, Ducker McLean chose to stay in the boat and was carried as a passenger to defeat.

By the time the Club celebrated its Silver Jubilee, Vincent's had a South African president, Herbert Hayton (known as 'H H') Castens, president in 1887. Castens did not shine especially at sport as an undergraduate, although he got one Blue in cricket, but in the next few years he became the first captain of both cricket and rugby for South Africa. His greatest innings is usually placed on Christmas Day 1884, but it was actually a Boxing Day that saw the bulk of it, when he scored 165 (139 not out on Boxing Day itself) in Cape Town. In rugby, he played for Villagers; he refereed the first provincial match of the first tour now recognised as being by the British & Irish Lions, and he played as captain in the first Test match, reverting to refereeing for the last Test. He then captained South Africa for cricket on their team's first tour of England, playing against W G Grace of Gloucestershire. Grace took nine wickets in the first innings and scored a century. Castens went on to be a senior civil servant in the old Rhodesia.

In every era, it is not only the Vincent's presidents or the most sporting of its membership who can proceed to a notable career. As the 1880s gave way to the 1890s, an 'ordinary' member of Vincent's was reflecting on the pertinent themes of social change and yet tradition. John Galsworthy of New College became a Vincent's member in Michaelmas 1889 and is the only Vincent's alumnus to have become a Nobel Laureate, winning the Nobel Prize for Literature in 1932. Galsworthy was captain of football at Harrow and enjoyed field sports as an undergraduate, despite having poor eyesight, but avoided more strenuous sport at Oxford, claiming a strained heart. He once explained that people with his upbringing, including being 'addicted to sport and travel', were unlikely to take literature seriously. In later life, he seemed to enjoy playing cricket more and more. He famously featured the Lord's cricket ground in his Forsyte saga, albeit as a place primarily for eating, drinking, meeting, seeing and being seen. The Nobel citation was for 'his distinguished art of narration, which takes its highest form in *The Forsyte Saga*'. Galsworthy did not make great claims for the deeper meaning of his work, but he spells out the symbolism in his account of society's revival after the First World War, albeit the Eton v Harrow game rather than Oxford v Cambridge:

> Lord's – that festival which the War had driven from the field – raised its light and dark blue flags for the second time, displaying almost every feature of a glorious past … There was life in the old dog yet! Tradition! And again Tradition! How strong and how elastic! Wars might rage, taxation prey, Trades Unions take their toll, and Europe perish of starvation; but the ten thousand would be fed; and, within their ring fence, stroll upon green turf, wear their top hats, and meet – themselves.

The 1890s began with Guy Nickalls as president, one of the greatest rowers of all time. When winning his first Blue, he was appalled at the tactics of the coach and at Ducker McLean's refusal to jump. He entitled his memoirs *Life's a Pudding*, although not because he liked a pudding, even though he put on four stones, a third of his bodyweight, on retiring from rowing. He shed the weight in his 40s when answering the country's call to oars in the London 1908 Olympics. He was needed because the Belgian crew were feared to be set for victory whereas, as Nickalls wrote, he had never been beaten by a Belgian or a colonial and he had no intention of starting now. The final was his last race. He won gold. It was at Henley, and Vincent's founder, W B Woodgate, was watching. He was not impressed with the form of the Olympics which he compared unfavourably to earlier Henley Regattas.

Nickalls' book title came instead from a song recalled from his undergraduate days. He had many undergraduate days to choose from, having ploughed Mods and Schools with equal facility and thus having spent five years winning Blues. When he was Vincent's president in 1890, six years before the Olympics were revived, number one in the hit parade was still the show which had opened in December 1889, Gilbert & Sullivan's *The Gondoliers*, very popular with rowers, which included these lines, albeit not one after the other as imagined in Nickalls' autobiography:

> Life's a pudding, full of plums …
> Let us take it as it comes

Nickalls is a good example not only of that relaxed approach to life but of the impossibility of containing Vincent's men within a structure of decades or eras. He went on from winning Olympic gold in his 40s, to anticipate slightly the next chapter, to insisting, when war broke out, on enlisting in the army in his 50s, initially as a physical training instructor in France, memorably and successfully taking on three enemy planes just with his rifle. In between times, Nickalls was coaching Yale crews and never lost confidence in his own considerable abilities. He wrote of another Vincent's rower who won gold in that 1908 crew, also in his last race: 'I think F S Kelly was most likely the fastest sculler of all time – quick, neat and polished. He was at his best in 1905, when he cut the record for the Diamonds. I think the advice I gave him had something to do with it.'

In 1896 Vincent's president was Henry Dudley Gresham (known as 'Shrimp') Leveson-Gower, a cricketer, selector, writer and compulsive organiser of teams. He captained Oxford and England before becoming a Test selector. He took sides to play against both Oxford and Cambridge as well as in the Scarborough Festival against touring sides. This gave him a unique perspective on varsity cricket. He valued his presidency of Vincent's and left Oxford without a degree to complement his Blues. He was captain in one of two varsity games in quick succession where Cambridge were considered by others to have played against the spirit of the game, which led to a change in the law about declarations.

Of the four University Matches in which I took part, those of 1893 and 1896 provided 'incidents'. In 1893 C M Wells and in 1896 E B Shine gave away eight runs while bowling, to prevent Oxford following on. Being captain at Oxford in 1896 I was naturally very interested in the decision reached by Frank Mitchell in giving orders to E B Shine to bowl no-balls to the boundary in order to prevent my side from going in again. In my opinion the reception he and his team received from the members of the MCC and, when his team went in to bat, from the spectators, was quite unjustifiable.

At the time, following on was compulsory. In 1896, Oxford won and Leveson-Gower could take some of the credit for one of the more subtle arts of the great varsity captains, selection. On the morning of the game, G B Raikes was expected to play but Leveson-Gower inspected the wicket and decided that Raikes' all-round abilities, including his bowling, would not be so vital as G O Smith's batting. So he made a bold decision between the two old Blues and fellow Vincent's members, plumping for Smith, a famous footballer. Oxford had to score 330 to win. Smith's 132 was a vindication of his captain's judgment. A spectator also wrote to thank Leveson-Gower for his curt insistence, during the lunch interval, that Oxford would win, despite the prospects looking bleak. He had asked because he had been offered odds of eight to one. To get rid of him, Leveson-Gower sounded more confident than he was, but the spectator was delighted with what he took to be inside information. Woodgate would have approved of this exchange, at least if he had liked cricket, which he did not.

This was a golden period of Oxford cricketers, rather perhaps than of Oxford cricket, for at least a hat-trick of other Vincent's members of the 1890s shone even more in their cricket after their University days. C B Fry was a better cricketer, cricket-writer and sporting all-rounder not only than Sir Harry D G Leveson-Gower, but as compared to almost anyone ever. While Fry's manifold sporting achievements were obvious, the other two, W H Brain and B J T Bosanquet, are of particular interest to those whose pioneering cricket preferences relate to the more subtle arts of out-thinking batsmen. Brain was not a great batsman himself. He was one of the last pair in one of those controversial games against Cambridge, when the Oxford tail-enders were conferring as to the advantages of getting out deliberately so that Oxford had to follow on, which is what led to Cambridge bowling deliberately to give extras away.

As a wicket-keeper, W H Brain was so pioneering that he is the only person in history to have pulled off an extraordinary feat, a hat-trick of stumpings in first-class cricket. He is the answer to a question raised in *Zimmer Men* by Marcus Berkmann, who was at Brasenose in the early 1980s and the co-founder of a cricket team for those who could not find a place in the College second team. Berkmann asked several questions himself, to which Brain was not the answer, such as, by way of explanation for the team: 'Surely there was a role for the athletically challenged, for the thin and coordinated, for the partially sighted, the overweight and the inert?' Is there a deep meaning to *Zimmer Men*? Not according to Berkmann, who asks and answers an even more searching question: 'I suppose the big question is: what do we learn from any of this? And the obvious answer is: nothing, absolutely nothing.' And yet his writing gives many reasons for believing the opposite. Statistics, for example, are a joy for many cricketers and followers of cricket. Where Brain features is when Berkmann talks in *Zimmer Men* of one of his long-standing team-mates, another Oxford alumnus, Richard Corden, becoming distracted when his spin bowling had surprisingly taken two wickets in successive balls, both stumped. He failed to get his hat-trick. What had bothered him? He had been trying to remember the name, with initials, of the only cricketer in the history of the first-class game to take a hat-trick of stumpings. He had to look up the answer overnight and straightaway emailed Berkmann with the answer.

It was W H Brain, for Gloucestershire against Somerset at Cheltenham in 1893. The bowler was the 16 year-old C L Townsend. Brain's other stumping earlier in that Somerset second innings was off the bowling of W G Grace. Gloucestershire still lost the match. Berkmann omits to mention the university where the wonderfully named Brain studied. To be specific, William Henry Brain was at Oriel. He came from a famous cricketing and brewing family, succeeding his cousin, the founder of the company, as chairman of Brains, the Cardiff brewery, which supported Glamorgan as it developed from minor county status to first class in 1921. Brains are known now also as sponsors of Welsh rugby.

William Henry Brain played initially for Gloucestershire, having been a schoolboy at Clifton College, but then played for Glamorgan and served the club in other ways in his later years. His Wisden obituary in 1934 records that he 'did much to help promote Glamorgan to first-class status'. Brain was also a Blue in football as the goalkeeper in the 1891/2 season, losing to Cambridge 5-1.

The Founder, Walter Bradford Woodgate, in typically idiosyncratic attire. (1)

Vincent's Club group photograph, 1889. (2)

Above: *Cecil Rhodes (1853–1902), founder of the Rhodes Scholarships programme. (3)*

Left: *The Club interior, c.1889. (4)*

Artist's sketch of Oxford v Cambridge athletics match, March 1891, from The Illustrated London News. *Oxford's P R Lloyd (Pembroke) is shown winning the 440 yards.* **(5)**

By the 1890s, University athletes and sportsmen were getting national recognition through The Illustrated London News *and its famous cartoonist 'Spy' (Sir Leslie Ward).*

Above: *'Flea' (William Alfred Littledale Fletcher), 'Spy' cartoon, 1893.* **(5a)**

The Earl of Rosebery (1847–1929). **(6)**

Bernard Bosanquet (1877–1936), Middlesex and England, inventor of the googly, photographed here in 1905. **(7)**

Sir Edward Grey (1862–1933), Foreign Secretary (1905–16). (8)

King Edward VII (1841–1910), centre, with his son Prince George (later George V), left, and his grandson Prince Edward (later Edward VIII), in 1909. Both Edwards were Vincent's members. (9)

Three cricket captains: South Africa, England and Australia. L to R Frank Mitchell (South Africa), C B Fry (England), Syd Gregory (Australia). Lord's, May 1912. Fry was thought by many to be 'the greatest all-rounder in Vincent's history'. (10)

Great Britain's Arnold Jackson (l) wins gold in the 1500 metres at the Stockholm Olympics, 1912. (11)

Dr Robert Bridges (1844–1930), distinguished rowing coach, physician and, later (from 1913), Poet Laureate. (12)

Left: Captain Noel Godfrey Chavasse VC and bar (1884–1917), one of only three men to be awarded the Victoria Cross twice (1916 and 1917). *(13)*

Right: Captain (later Revd) Geoffrey Harold Woolley VC (1892–1968), the first Territorial Army officer to be awarded the Victoria Cross (1915). *(14)*

Far left: George Mallory and Andrew Irvine at base camp, Nepal, 1924 Mount Everest Expedition. *(15)*

Left: Bevil Rudd (1894–1948) of South Africa, gold medallist in the 400 metres at the Antwerp Olympics, 1920. *(16)*

Sir Pelham 'Plum' Warner, captain of England 1903–6, and grand old man of English cricket, on his retirement as captain of Middlesex in 1920. (17)

Guy 'Gully' Oliver Nickalls (1899–1974), rowing for Oxford, March 1921. (18)

Lord Curzon, 1921, Viceroy of India
(1899–1905) and Foreign Secretary
(1919–24). (19)

Three generations of the Browne family who served as
Club stewards for Vincent's first 59 years. (20)

*Left: John Galsworthy
(1867–1933), Nobel
Prize for Literature in
1932. (21)*

Below: *Mile of the
Century, 1935. Jack
Lovelock (New Zealand)
celebrates victory over
the best of the US milers
at Palmer Stadium,
Princeton University,
Princeton, NJ. (22)*

Above: *Two captains: Bill Woodfull (l), Australia, and
Douglas Jardine (r), England. Fifth Test, Australia v England,
the notorious 'Bodyline Tour', 1933. (23)*

Prince Alexander Obolensky
in action, October 1937. *(24)*

Above: Airey Neave (1916–79), Vincent's member 1935–8, distinguished soldier in World War Two, successful escapee from Colditz, subsequently barrister and MP, and assassinated by the IRA in the Houses of Parliament in 1979. *(25)*

Tony Pawson, Oxford University first XI, Oxford University v Lancashire, second day, 1947. *(26)*

Left: Martin Donnelly (1917–99) represented New Zealand at cricket and England at rugby. *(27)*

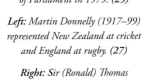

Right: Sir (Ronald) Thomas ('Tommy') Stewart Macpherson CBE, MC and two bars, TD and DL, war hero who among many other exploits personally engineered the surrender of 23,000 German soldiers after the Normandy landings in 1944. *(28)*

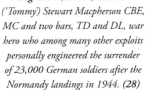

Far left: Major Sir Wilfred Thesiger CBE, DSO, FRAS, FRGS (1910–2003), graduated in 1933 having won Blues in boxing for all four years at Oxford. A distinguished explorer and soldier, he became a much-published authority on the Arabian peninsula and Iraq. *(29)*

Left: M J K Smith, Oxford and Warwickshire. *(30)*

Above: Roger Bannister crosses
the line in the world's first sub-
four-minute mile
(3 mins 59.6 seconds),
6 May 1954. *(31)*

Right: Roger Bannister (r)
and Christopher Chataway (l)
pictured holding their awards,
1954. Bannister was Sports
Illustrated Sportsman of the Year
and Chataway was BBC Sports
Personality of the Year. *(32)*

Rather than the goalie being blamed, it was the next person on the team-sheet, a freshman, who was held responsible for the defeat. Colin Weir, in *The History of Oxford United Association Football Club 1872–1998,* does not draw particular attention to W H Brain being in goal but does note of the right-back that his 'fancy kicking' let in Cambridge to score twice early on. The right-back's name was C B Fry of Wadham, soon to become famous for equalling the world long-jump record as a student, as well as for his prowess in cricket, football and rugby.

Another detail of Brain's pioneering spirit has only recently come to light. As wicket-keepers will often do, Brain took custody of the ball at the end of that match between Gloucestershire and Somerset. The custom is to let the bowler of the hat-trick keep the ball but, given the youth of Townsend, Brain first had it mounted with an inscription, then he presented the bowler with it. The ball remained in the cricketing Townsend family, with impeccable provenance, until much of their memorabilia was auctioned, including this trophy. So Brain's focus in 1893 was on the bowler, whom he had assisted, rather than on his own record, which has never been equalled in 120 years anywhere in the world.

To check that, or any other claim, we are very familiar nowadays with the word 'Google', both as a noun and a verb. The standard explanation is that it is a variation on the theme of 'googol', a word invented for the number represented by one followed by 100 zeros, with the happy coincidence that it is the combination of 'go' and 'ogle' and, perhaps above all, that the domain name was available. There is another element, however, which is the cricketing term 'googly', incorporated into wider discourse as indicating a tricky question. The Oxford English Dictionary traces 'google', as a verb for bowling googlies, back to 1907. It could be said that many a leg-break bowler could have registered 'google' for a website or blog but failed to foresee the turn of events.

In cricket, to bowl a googly is to bowl a delivery which looks like a leg-break but actually turns the opposite way, like an off-break. The hand, wrist and arm seem to be in the same position as for the leg-break but the ball spins in the opposite direction. This is achieved by turning the wrist sufficiently to alter the axis of spin. With a right-arm bowler and batsman, the standard leg-break moves away from the batsman, towards the wicket-keeper, slips and gully but the off-break spins back into the batsman, ideally surprising the batsman and hitting the stumps. One explanation for the term 'googly' is that it leaves the batsman 'google-eyed'.

The pioneer of the deliberate googly is almost universally recognised as Vincent's Bernard James Tindall Bosanquet, nephew of an Oxford philosopher, also called Bernard, and father of an Oxford television newsreader called Reginald Bosanquet. Our Bosanquet played other sports from ice hockey to tennis, and might well have been helped in his discovery of the googly by representing Oxford in an unusual ABC of varsity sport: athletics, billiards and cricket. He was a hammer-thrower, which must have helped his understanding of rotation and swing, as must the application of spin in billiards. At Oxford, he was a medium-paced bowler and batsman but: 'Somewhere about the year 1897 I was playing a game with a tennis ball, known as "Twist-Twosti". The object was to bounce the ball on a table so that your opponent sitting opposite could not catch it.' It is not recorded whether playing so much sport and experimenting at Twisti-Twosti is why he left Oriel without taking his degree, but he practised assiduously in the nets and tried the delivery on an American tour and in a county game before unleashing it against the Australians at home in 1902 and away in 1903.

The reason why it retained the element of surprise is the same reason why some people point to earlier 'googlies'. The mysteries of the art of the leg-break bowler include sometimes bowling a googly by accident, when trying to spin the ball more vigorously. The first few Australians were puzzled that these 'accidents' were pitching in the right place to get them out, but eventually it dawned on batsmen that Bosanquet was doing it deliberately. Actually, they were helped by his captain at Oxford and in later life, 'Plum' Warner, who was also a journalist and could not resist writing the story. In honour of Bosanquet, Australians called the delivery a Bosie or Bosey. It is also known as the 'wrong 'un'. That last term captures the element of deception which, together with the potential for puns on turn or spin, explains why the word 'googly' has sometimes been used in politics and the media to describe a question which tricks or otherwise surprises the person being asked.

Between the Club's Silver Jubilee in 1888 and its Golden Jubilee in 1913, relations between Britain and South Africa might have ruptured the supply lines of inspiration, but perhaps the sporting exchanges, and the business and political connections of Cecil Rhodes and his friends, kept those connections open. A year after Castens' exciting Christmas, Lord Hawke brought out an XI, the equivalent of an MCC tour. This was the one and only overseas tour by C B Fry, who some think was the greatest all-rounder in Vincent's history. On Christmas Day 1885, he tried to climb up Table Mountain. On Boxing Day, you might see in some sources that he took ten wickets. He did take ten in the match, five in each innings, although the opposition had 16 batsmen. Western Province organised an extra one-day game and then the visitors headed towards Johannesburg as 1895 gave way to 1896. Meanwhile, the Jameson Raid was heading from the north to the same destination. Fry was a little scared when the touring cricketers' train was stopped and those holding up the train declined his peace offering of a cricket match, saying that they didn't play cricket but they did shoot. Eventually, it emerged that they were not threatening to shoot Fry, Hawke and co[mpany] but to compete against them in shooting animals and birds. Fry got injured twice on tour, once playing a form of polo against Hussars, the cricketers in fact playing hockey on their feet while the soldiers played polo on horseback. Not surprisingly, as with cross-code games of rugby, this produced mayhem when horses tackled or slammed into cricketers. Fry recovered to go riding in early March, only for his horse to bolt; he was thrown and broke his leg. This is my preferred explanation for one of sport's great mysteries: why did Fry, who also played football for England, won rugby Cuppers with Wadham, and was the joint world-record holder in the long jump, not go to the Athens 1896 Olympics, which were held that Easter? One answer is: because he was injured in South Africa.

To consider another possibility, to appreciate Fry's world record in the long jump and to ponder why Vincent's was under-represented at the 1896 Athens Olympics, it is worth contemplating the 1894 Wadham rugby three-quarters of C B Fry, A A Roche, John Simon and F E Smith. This Wadham team won Cuppers and then played the Tab champions, Caius, beating them also in an away match and wrecking a railway carriage on the return journey, for which the captain F E Smith was fined £20. Fry and Smith tried out for the Blues. Fry played several times although it was his fourth sport, after being a world-class athlete, Test match cricketer and England international at football. He played rugby for Oxford, Blackheath and the Barbarians but was injured a fortnight before the varsity match. He was still selected and declared himself fit but the captain decided he was not fit enough to play. He could not, by all accounts, including his own, tackle, but he was undoubtedly a fast runner. Beyond sport, Fry, a Vincent's member, had the least illustrious career of the quarter. Roche became a Law Lord, a senior judge. Smith and Simon both became Lord Chancellor, at the time the most senior judge. Smith and Simon both got Firsts, and both were president of the Union. Simon was a Fellow of All Souls and held all the high offices of state apart from being Prime Minister. Smith put not gaining his rugby Blue as the biggest disappointment of his life.

C B Fry is one of the few people to have 'scholar, athlete' on his gravestone. This is a new headstone at Repton School's churchyard, which describes him in two lines as, first, 'Cricketer, Scholar, Athlete, Author' and then, underneath that, as, 'The Ultimate All Rounder'. His claims as a scholar rest on having beaten F E Smith in the Wadham entrance procedure and in achieving a First in Classics Moderations. A Fourth in Final Honours Schools, however, could be counted against him although Blessed John Henry Newman recovered from poor results in Finals to become a scholar of substance. Fry did not pursue a scholarly path after Oxford and was no saint. (Newman was no athlete.) Fry was prolific as a journalist and had other achievements of note on and off the cricket field but his scholarship cannot stand comparison with, say, that of Arthur Johnson, Vincent's FA Cup winner, or even Warden Pember, who did not write much at All Souls. Fry's fame, his life's work educating youngsters on a training ship, his prolific output as a journalist and his role in the higher echelons of cricket could have led to some honours, albeit not as great as those of his fellow winners of Cuppers, but he was seen in the 1930s as far too sympathetic to the Nazi emphasis on sport, appreciating too late the horrors of Hitler's regime.

At the highest level of sport, he is one of two Vincent's athletes to have left their world mark on these first 50 years of the Club, following Marshall Brooks' world high-jump record two decades before.

Even if Fry was denied the glory of Olympic gold, he extracted the maximum interest from his world record earlier in this decade, in March 1893. Fry has benefited from several hagiographies, some from himself. Denzil Batchelor repeats some of Fry's embellishments of the circumstances of his long-jump record but is on surer ground when observing that between the turn of the century and the First World War, 'all through those years Charles Fry was the greatest run-getting machine in cricket' and he did so under a media scrutiny akin to that experienced by a modern-day sports star:

Charles Fry was the first of his kind to have a non-stop spotlight turned on him. What he did was always news. The posters said Fry Again or Fry Fails. Whichever way it went, from Oxford onwards the public wanted to know all about what had happened to him. In this sense, he pioneered the life in the media of the modern professional sportsman, while clinging on to his amateur status and yet writing about the sport in which he was participating – the consummate all-rounder.

Ellis is more circumspect, noting that Fry 'was never one to miss the opportunity for decorating stories with increasingly implausible flourishes' and dismissing legends as to whether Fry was smoking a cigar between leaps. Instead, he sets out the facts, which are impressive enough. The world record

had been set up by the American C S Reber at Detroit in 1891. The setting was Iffley Road in Oxford, where the university's internal sports were held on 4 and 6 March 1893 ... for some reason which remained a mystery to both athlete and spectators he achieved more spring than usual and gained exceptional height, probably three feet off the ground at the highest point in the leap. He remembered that he did not have the usual problem of struggling for his balance when he landed in an attempt to avoid falling back. He bounced clean out of the pit and landed six feet away on the track. A broad grin gave notice to the enthusiastic crowd that he had done something extraordinary and the tape-measure confirmed it .... A contemporary account in The Oxford Magazine ... described the enormous impact made by Fry in his first eighteen months at the university ... 'Fry remains a notable example of what athletes were in the palmiest days of the Greek games'.

Hence it would indeed have been the perfect opportunity for Fry to live up to this judgment if he had been a competitor in Athens. Resisting hitherto the common claim that Vincent's and the Union were at daggers drawn, it might be that the 1896 Olympics is one example where it did matter that the two student societies were not closer in spirit. For another explanation as to Fry's absence would be that even if he were not playing cricket in South Africa or breaking his leg, he would have been hard pressed to learn that the Games were happening unless he had happened to be at the Union or to have seen there a notice of a talk by a Balliol student, Constantine Manou, who was one of the organisers and who was encouraging (rather ineffectually and at the wrong place, Vincent's members might have said) participation from Oxford students, at their own expense, in this pioneering revival. George Robertson, later Sir George Robertson QC, a Blue and multiple University prize-winning classical scholar of Magdalen, saw the notice and went along to Athens, not doing too well in the sport but composing the ode that he recited at the end of the Games, much to the bemusement of the Greek king and his entourage who struggled to understand Robertson's accent. Manou's friend, John Pius (known as 'Jack') Boland of Christ Church went along to watch and ended up winning tennis gold in the singles and doubles, often therefore being counted as Ireland's and sometimes Britain's first Olympic champion. Neither was a Vincent's member, however, and if only Manou had walked a little further than the Union, there might have been a better response to his plea for students to compete.

There was, however, no shortage of adventure on and off the sports pitches of the world for Vincent's members in the 1890s and beyond. Moreover, Fry and one of the last members elected in the 19th century, John Buchan of Brasenose, are good examples of an objection which might be made about any account of individuals who happened to be Vincent's members. Would they not have shone in sport and life anyway, whether or not they were members of Vincent's or of any other club or society? After all, Fry had Wadham and his College, University, county, club and international teams. The influence of Vincent's is unquantifiable, but it is certainly the case that Fry and Buchan were 'clubbable', in that they sought company beyond their colleges. Fry found athletics after University to be unedifying as it lacked that club element which he found in football for Southampton, including in an FA Cup Final of his own, and in county and Test cricket. By bringing together outstanding students in diverse sports and those who had other interests, Vincent's added a different slice of University friends to the experience of its members, as well as adding a lustre among those who recognised the distinction of being elected.

To illustrate the fun side of all this and the deadly serious aspect of what was to come, there is a story told by Fry which we can but wish is true. It links, 20 years later, two Vincent's undergraduates of these 1890s and shows how people were all-rounders, from a clergyman at war to a Test batsman at play in club cricket. Bishop Walter Carey went up to Oxford in 1894, to Hertford College because a teacher had told Clement Jackson that Carey could row. He did row for the college boat but concentrated at university level on rugby, winning four Blues:

'I was in the swim of Oxford life – four years a blue, captain of my college boat, on the committee of Vincent's'. Two decades later, he was on a boat, in the Battle of Jutland. Soon afterwards, C B Fry came across another boat from that battle. Writing the preface to a book celebrating village cricket, Fry had the good grace to say that the last time he had played at such a level he was out for a duck and then to recall that

> During the 1914–18 war I had the luck to play in a match on the RN ground at Devonport. HMS *Barham* was alongside just beyond the iron rails of the boundary and I hooked a short ball on to the deck and the ball went down a hole made by a German shell at Jutland, so I rank that with stardom.

Carey, known in sport for coining the Barbarians' motto, 'Rugby football is a game for gentlemen in all classes but for no bad sportsman in any class'. In his memoir, *Good-bye To My Generation*, his variation on that theme is that at Oxford he learned 'true sportsmanship: win if you can, but if you lose take it gracefully'.

As the century came to a close, and ten years after Galsworthy, John Buchan of Brasenose became a member in 1899 and could still be seen as Vincent's second-string author to the Nobel Laureate. He dedicated his most famous book, *The Thirty-Nine Steps*, to his friend and to Vincent's last president of the 19th century, the Scottish rugby player Tommy Nelson. Buchan joined the Nelson family business in publishing and worked with Tommy, although Nelson were not the publishers of this particular book, which Buchan completed soon after the First World War started in 1914, while suffering from a duodenal ulcer. When recovered, he joined the army and worked in Intelligence later in the Great War, eventually living to the time of the Second World War. He became an MP and then Governor-General of Canada. *The Thirty-Nine Steps* was published in 1915. The film by Alfred Hitchcock in 1935 confirmed Buchan's fame and the book, dedicated to the Vincent's president of 1899, who died in the First World War, is sometimes described as the first spy novel. Buchan was not precious about his writing, which was necessary to make a living, and thought that Hitchcock had greatly improved on the novel in adapting it for cinema.

E D H Sewell's account of Scottish rugby heroes who died in the First World War explains that Captain Thomas Nelson of the 1st Lothians and Border Horse went to France in September 1915 and was mentioned in despatches three times, 30 April 1916; 13 November 1916; and 9 April 1917. The last of these was for his actions on the day he was killed by a shell while acting as an observation officer for the tanks. John Buchan, by now a colonel in Intelligence, wrote in *The Times*:

> ... the great publishing house which bears his name ... grew to be perhaps the largest organization of its kind in the world. But his life could not be narrowed to one interest .... He had a deep interest in all schemes of social betterment, and, being too modest to preach, he was content to practise ... He was the best of sportsmen, not merely because he did everything well and with immense gusto, but because he had in his bones the love of wild life and adventure and contest. But his great endowment was his genius for friendship with all human classes and conditions.

Nelson's immediate successor as president of Vincent's in 1900 was Reginald Erskine 'Tip' Foster. What a sportsman to have as the president of Vincent's at the turn of the century! He had come up to University College in 1896. His first three Blues followed in 1897 in golf, rackets and cricket. Foster also participated in college rowing and athletics. The following year, he played for the Oxford football team. Foster is still the record-holder for a Test debut score in Australia and for the highest innings in Australia of any England batsman. Foster's family were all sporting – father, mother, six brothers and three sisters. There is a website dedicated to the family, which records that the seven boys scored 42,000 first-class runs between them. Three were Oxford Blues. The family, including the sisters, enjoyed playing an annual Boxing Day game of cricket against the rest of their county, Worcestershire.

Tip Foster was not only a quadruple Blue but his degree was a Fourth and he has a further quartet of claims to fame. Jeremy Malies in his book *Sporting Doubles* gives more detail on Tip Foster. First, he is the only person in history to have captained the full England teams at cricket and football. Second, he is the only person in history to have hit four sixes in an over bowled by W G Grace, which he did in 1900, in the Parks, against Grace's London County side, while scoring 169. Third, he scored six goals for England (amateurs) in a single game against Germany (their first international fixture, which England won 12-0 at

White Hart Lane). C B Fry's judgment of him as a soccer player was that, 'his feet had, as it were, the Oxford accent'. Fry was well placed to make that judgment. In 1901, for instance, when Foster scored the third goal in England's victory over Ireland, Fry was one half of the best long-jumping pair of Oxford Blue and international full backs in history, the other being William Oakley of Christ Church, who also captained England in that one game. Fourth, Tip Foster ought to be best known – as 2013–14 sees two Ashes series, home and away, and given double centuries recently by Cook and Pietersen – for still holding the record score for an English player in the Ashes in Australia, his 287 on his Test debut at Sydney in 1903. Yet although it was often mentioned in media reports of England's last Australian tour that even Cook's astonishing form left him behind Wally Hammond's record *total* for an Ashes series, Foster's highest individual score rarely featured. This might be because Hammond is a better-known figure to cricket journalists, partly because he focused on cricket, partly because he was born later, partly because he lived a much longer life. Tip Foster struggled on the rest of that Australian tour with diabetes and died of his illness before the First World War, in May 1914, aged 36.

While Foster was setting a record in Australia in 1903, another Vincent's member, an Australian, was setting new standards in Oxford rowing and in Henley sculling, who went on to win gold with Guy Nickalls in the London 1908 eight. Unlike Guy Nickalls, F S Kelly was not against Continentals or Colonials, having lived in Frankfurt for years, honing his craft as a classical pianist and composer, and being colonial himself, an Australian.

The story can be found in *Race Against Time – The Diaries of F S Kelly*, published in 2004, selected, edited and introduced by Thérèse Radic. 'Sep' or 'Cleg' Kelly was a musical scholar at Balliol. He won the Diamond Challenge Sculls at Henley in 1902. He won his Blue in 1903 but lost the Boat Race. He won the Diamond Sculls again in 1903 but lost in a heat in the Diamonds in 1904. Lou F Scholes of Toronto was two lengths behind Kelly but put on a spurt and went past him. At the Grand Stand, Kelly was two lengths behind and, totally exhausted, had to stop and be lifted out of the water. Sir Theodore Cook wrote that Kelly had not trained for long enough that summer. In 1905, he returned to win. Although Scholes was not competing, Kelly won in eight minutes, ten seconds, beating Scholes' 1904 time by 13 seconds, a record that lasted until 1938.

Kelly's father had died in 1901, his mother in 1902 and he graduated with a Fourth in History in 1903 before going to Frankfurt to study music. He read *The Times* in a café there five years later about his old rival, Scholes, and the prospect of the Olympic rowing in Henley at the end of July 1908. Kelly was not selected for the sculls and Scholes lost in his first heat but Kelly was chosen for the Leander eight, Britain's second boat, the first being Cambridge. Kelly and Leander won the Olympic gold in the eights. The final was Kelly's last rowing race.

Only weeks later, *The Complete Oarsman* was published by R C Lehmann, who explained elegantly that the section on sculling was written by, 'Mr. F S Kelly, the master of the art'. As we come towards the end of Vincent's first 50 years, Kelly's brilliant chapter can serve as an example of the contribution of many members to developing their sports, and to understanding wider life. Some devoted years to coaching Oxford and other crews and teams. Others wrote books and newspaper articles. Several did both. In this gem of an essay, Kelly makes at least five points of ever-broader interest. First, he explains how to scull:

> SCULLING, in its essentials, does not differ from rowing ... The functions of a perfect style in sculling are twofold. (A) The most effective use of the weight and strength of the sculler for a continuous application of both in those parts of the stroke which propel the boat, i.e. when the blades are in the water. (B) The accomplishment of those motions, whose function it is to prepare the body for the next propelling part of the stroke, with the least possible expenditure of strength, and yet with as great a celerity as is compatible, not only with the necessity for some recuperation of the wind and muscles, but with the almost greater desirability that, when these motions are completed, the body shall be under sufficient control to start once more upon the propelling portion of the stroke without loss of time.

Next, it is worth considering whether his fundamental advice on race tactics applies to other sports, such as the quest to run the mile in under four minutes:

CHAPTER 2 • 1863–1913: THE PIONEERS

It may sound paradoxical to say that it is not by sculling his hardest that a man goes fastest, but it is undoubtedly a fact that if, in a full course, all his strength is expended in the desire to accomplish the half course in the fastest possible time, he will accomplish the remaining half of the course at such a lamentably slow pace that the fast time for the first half and the slow time for the second half, when added together, will be considerably in excess of the time he would have done, had he been content to reach the halfway mark several seconds slower, sculling hard yet without reducing himself almost to a standstill. The strength, in this course as in the others, should be entirely exhausted by the time the finishing post is reached, not by its excessive application at any particular point of the course, but rather by its gradual expenditure during the entire distance.

Third, Kelly showed that he had learned from his own defeat:

Sculling races differ from rowing races in the fact that in the former there frequently comes a period when a sculler, who is really hard pressed, undergoes a complete collapse and is incapable of finishing the course, whereas a crew of oarsmen nearly always manages to reach the winning-post somehow, even if they have long before been at their last gasp. Whatever may be the reason of this, it is an important fact to bear in mind when engaged in a sculling race, and every sculler should beware of approaching that extreme of exhaustion, bordering on collapse, without very good cause.

Fourth, he explores how a better opponent might be beaten, a lesson which could apply to other sports and perhaps to life beyond sport, with appropriate adjustments for military or economic competition, as the world prepared for war:

Advice, however, cannot be offered as to how a sculler may win a race against an opponent who is faster than himself. Such races have been won, and the result is due to the possession by the winner of a sort of genius, akin to that of a good stroke in rowing, which cannot be wholly taught. This genius makes its possessor instinctively aware of his opponent's weak spots, and, as he cannot win by continuous pace alone, his only tactics are to judge at what part of the course a sudden increase in his own pace is most likely to unsettle his opponent, and to stake every thing on this extra effort: or he may, perhaps, begin spurting before the first minute is over so as to prevent his opponent from settling down into his stride, in the hopes that, by taking him out of his pace at whatever cost to himself, his opponent may be the first to 'crack.' At what part of the course, though, this extra pressure should be exerted is a question which must be decided anew in every race, and the more experience a sculler has of racing the more likely is he to choose the moment.

Finally, Kelly reminds us, as someone who had won and lost and then won again at the highest levels of his sport, how to bounce back from disappointment by taking responsibility oneself:

> In sculling, as in every other form of sport or game, every man has what are known as 'off days', in which his skill seems unaccountably to desert him, and during such periods he should beware of over-haste in seeking for external causes.

Indeed, it is an engaging feature of so many recollections by Vincent's members that they do not rush to blame others for their losses or for not being selected, as illustrated by G D 'Khaki' Roberts QC. In his memoir *Without My Wig*, written in the 1950s, Roberts refers to his 1909 Final examination in Torts, a copy of which he had in front of him, and to being dropped from the team for Twickenham in 1905. Roberts was well known for being selected for England before getting his rugby Blue and for being one of the leading counsel for the prosecution at Nuremberg. Of the Oxford rugby selectors' rejection of him as a freshman, then England recognising the merits of his case, his tutor, a famous academic lawyer and legal historian, William Holdsworth (later Professor Sir William Holdsworth OM, KC, FBA), said that it was like the King's Bench Division being overruled by the Court of Appeal. Roberts himself thought it might have had something to do with playing badly in Oxford's 47-0 defeat by the All Blacks just before the varsity match. He was pleased to get a half-Blue for tennis doubles and then his rugby Blue. He did not think that he played that badly against the All Blacks but said that it looked to the selectors as if he must have been the one to blame for some trouble as he was the one left after a fracas on the pitch with the 'all-black eye'.

That 1909 Torts paper in the Oxford Final Honours School of Jurisprudence asked in question 9 whether a character 'A' had any remedies in law in various circumstances including, in part (c), this indication of the changing world:

9 Has A any and if so what remedy in the following cases?

… (c) He is lunching in his room which opens on to his garden. He sees a local Socialist walking up and down his gravel walk, occasionally stopping outside the window to stare unpleasantly at A's meal, and to make a few rude observations.

In that year, the Vincent's president was A G Kirby who won gold in the Stockholm 1912 Olympics in the same crew as another president, Ewart Horsfall, together with several other members of Vincent's, as the final was between a New College crew and a Leander crew that was Magdalen in disguise, with one substitute from Cambridge. Kirby, Horsfall and many others were to fight in the War that followed.

In 1910, Vincent's Phillip Le Couteur, who played for Oxford also in tennis and football, dominated the varsity cricket match, scoring 160 in Oxford's only innings, then taking six wickets for 20 runs in Cambridge's first innings and five for 46 in their second. Oxford won by an innings and 126 runs. He was an Australian Rhodes Scholar, a musician and a philosopher. He took eight for 99 in Cambridge's second innings the following year, once again spinning Oxford to victory.

R O Lagden, another whose wartime experiences will be mentioned in the next chapter, also took three wickets in Cambridge's first innings in Le Couteur's 1910 triumph. In 1911, while still a student, he played for England against Scotland at Twickenham. A number eight, Lagden converted two tries in the 13-8 victory; he became Vincent's president in 1912. An Oriel man, Lagden played in the varsity rackets once, the hockey twice, the rugby thrice and the cricket four times. In rugby, he had played in the great 1909 varsity game when Ronnie Poulton scored five tries. He taught at Harrow but was also in the Officer Training Corps at Oxford and volunteered as soon as war broke out.

At the Stockholm 1912 Olympics, Arnold Jackson, nephew of Clement, bowled up as a private citizen, interrupting his holiday, to the 1500 metres. Despite not being familiar with the metric distance, he glided through the heats, the first time he had run on a 400 metre or 440 yard track or run anti-clockwise (as Oxford's track was in those days one-third of a mile and the tradition was to run clockwise). He got the hang of it and won the final. Wearing his Oxford shorts, he strode to an Olympic record and added Strode- to his surname. His war medals could also consume the whole of the next chapter, but one of the bars on his DSO explains enough for an important point of relevance to each chapter: 'The machine-gun fire against them was intense, but the gallant leading of this officer gave such impetus to the assault that the enemy's main line of resistance was broken.' Under this kind of attack, Strode-Jackson was one of a number of Vincent's men whose injuries left him with a limp that prevented the resumption of his running but this did not stop him continuing to play a part in the Club and in Oxford sport in each of these three eras. He continued to offer advice in America and eventually, in retirement, back at Iffley Road and in Vincent's itself, right through to his death in 1972, 60 years after his Olympic gold.

King Edward VII and his grandson, who briefly became King Edward VIII before he abdicated, both studied at Oxford but only reached Olympian heights in the sense of Edward VII opening the London 1908 Olympic Games, and the later Edward VIII being present when his mother signalled the start of the marathon at Windsor. Edward VII was a student at Christ Church 1859–61. Edward VIII (as Prince of Wales) was a student at Magdalen in the run-up to the First World War. They both liked field sports. The Duke of Windsor wrote in his memoirs, *A King's Story* (Cassell, 1951), of his time at Magdalen in 1912–14, that Oxford was a serious place and that therefore his 'days by and large were sober, tranquil, and studious'. Not everyone agreed. Still, by his own account, when he did find time for relaxation: 'In the winter my leisure was given to football, beagling with the New College, Magdalen, and Trinity packs, and riding; in the summer I punted on the Cherwell and went for natural-history walks.' He enjoyed sporting celebrations, such as a bump supper in hall. He was also amused by the fact that, 'Whatever the occasion, Magdalen celebrations always ended the same way. Arms linked together, the celebrants would head for the president's house, to stand swaying under his bedroom window, chanting in chorus, "Well rowed, the Pree." Wholly apart from his literary leanings, Dr Warren's corpulence would have removed him from any conceivable athletic connection ...'. Dr Warren was an honorary member of Vincent's, in recognition of the sportsmen that Magdalen had brought to Oxford and the Club.

Other Oxford alumni of the pre-First World War era, such as Archbishop Lang already mentioned, were involved in the Prince of Wales's brief and difficult reign as King Edward VIII. In particular, his principal adviser over the abdication was Walter Monckton KC, a fellow Vincent's member, of whom he wrote, 'Our association had begun at Oxford, before the First World War', through the Officer Training Corps. Monckton had been appointed by the Prince of Wales as Attorney General to the Duchy of Cornwall and was knighted by him as King Edward VIII. Soon, however, he was being called upon to help the king negotiate with the Prime Minister (Stanley Baldwin, Trinity College, Cambridge) during what became the Abdication Crisis. Sir Walter (later Lord) Monckton was a good man for any crisis, from the sublime, with his Military Cross in the Great War, to the singular cricketing achievement, while batting at number eleven for Oxford and Cambridge Universities against the Army & Navy in his one and only first-class match, of scoring 29 not out in the first innings and 43 in the second to secure a first-class average of 72. That is not to say that Monckton emerged victorious from all crises. He did help win the War, but that cricket match was lost to the Army & Navy.

Moreover, as a schoolboy he had lost one of the most famous cricket matches in history. As Harrow's wicket-keeper in Fowler's match at Lord's in 1910, Monckton had seen Eton follow on and set his team only 54 to win, but Robert St Leger Fowler then took eight wickets, including clean bowling Monckton for a duck, as Eton dismissed Harrow for 45. So Monckton's team lost by nine runs in what Wisden asserted was the most sensational match in the whole history of cricket. Even a couple of years ago, on its centenary, this game was described in *The Spectator* as 'what might just be the greatest cricket match of all time'. Although Monckton was on the losing side in 1910 and in 1937, his conduct throughout the abdication crisis seems to have enhanced his reputation with all who were involved. Monckton (Balliol, president of the Union) was later Solicitor General and held other high office before accepting an hereditary peerage. He became the first Chancellor of the new University of Sussex ('Balliol-by-the-sea') and achieved a cricketing double in serving as president of Surrey CCC and of the MCC.

As Vincent's reached its jubilee year in 1913, the looming war dominated politics. Vincent's president in its 50th year was Robert Vickers (known as 'Roy') Bardsley, who played billiards for Oxford in 1911 and 1912, golf in 1913 and cricket in all three of those years. He became Governor of the Blue Nile region. In 1913, the brightest new sporting hope of the university was the freshman and South African Bevil Rudd, who won his first athletics Blue. He was to fight in the war, then return to become president of Vincent's and an extraordinary Olympian. One of the most established sportsmen of the era was David McLaren Bain. One account of his rugby prowess describes his achievements, while still a student, in these terms:

> David McLaren Bain played for Oxford against Cambridge in 1910, 1911, 1912, 1913, was Secretary of the Oxford University Rugby Union Club in 1912–13, and Captain in 1913–14 ... In March 1911 Bain made the first of eleven appearances for Scotland in the Calcutta Cup match at Twickenham. He played in every match for Scotland of the two years 1912 and 1913 against England, Wales, and France; against the South Africans in 1912; against Ireland in 1913 and 1914; and against Wales in 1914. Bain captained the Scots against Wales in 1914 ... Bain was one of those forwards one saw not very much of in the loose, which is generally a good sign, tending to mean that if he is any good at all he is very good. He was certainly a sure tackler good at the line-out, and with an excellent knowledge of the game .... Off the Rugby field at Oxford, he was a member of Vincent's in 1910, and President of it in 1913–14.

This chapter ends, however, as the next begins, with a Vincent's man from a previous era, Sir Edward Grey, who was the longest-serving Foreign Secretary in our history but who had also been secretary of Vincent's. In 1913, he was doing his utmost to avert the war which was to claim so many lives. He had been sent down by Balliol's famous Master, Dr Benjamin Jowett, who signed the following record in the minute-book for 19 January 1884:

> Sir Edward Grey, having been repeatedly admonished for idleness, and having shown himself entirely ignorant of the work set him in vacation as a condition of residence, was sent down, but allowed to come up to pass his examination in June.

By 1907 he had received an Honorary Doctorate of Civil Law from Oxford and his 1889 book *Fly Fishing* was in its fourth edition. By 1917, he had taken a peerage, having resigned from government because of his failing eyesight and could not even see to fish. In 1929 he became Chancellor of Oxford University, about which more will follow. In his sporting youth, however, he had won the two great real tennis championships, at Lord's and at Queen's. War began, and the next chapter begins, with a famous quotation from him as Foreign Secretary, but as he struggled to preserve the peace and to cope with his own developing disability, a fitting conclusion to this 50 years of Vincent's pioneers is to rediscover a passage in that masterpiece on fishing. Some individuals will recognise it in themselves, or come to do so. In this context, it also is a challenge for the Club itself. As each decade passes in a person or perhaps half a century in a club, we might reflect on whether we follow Grey's advice or whether we can defy the years:

As we grow older a change takes place. Let us analyse, for instance, the pleasure in games. At first we desire only to win – we think of that; we play the game as boys read an exciting story, with a feverish anxiety to know the end. The next stage, as we grow older, is more intelligent, and we begin to understand the qualities of good play. We improve year by year, and take pride in the increase of our own physical prowess, of which the limit is not yet seen. Then from understanding we pass to an artistic admiration of good play for its own sake; we become judges of how the thing should be done, and we are critics of style. Competition is then desired, not solely for the excitement it provides, but as a stimulus to good play; we no longer seriously expect to improve in our own play, but we take pleasure in doing our best. The last stage may be a long one; it begins with the admission that we are past our best. Strength is not diminished, and indeed we may even have more sheer strength than ever, but the effort of using it has become greater. The first sign of deterioration is seen when our powers seem as great, but it becomes more exhausting to use them, and when in a hard game we do not last so well. The next symptom follows very soon; we cannot do so quickly what can no longer be done so easily; our performance suggests retrospect; the personal element wanes, and we find satisfaction more and more in contemplation and less and less in excitement and competition; at last we sit among the onlookers, and are advised by our friends to practise golf.

CHAPTER 3

1913–1963: Heroes

The former Vincent's secretary, Sir Edward Grey, who had been the Foreign Secretary since 1905, famously looked out of the Foreign Office windows towards St James's Park at dusk on the evening of 3 August 1914 and said, 'The lamps are going out all over Europe; we shall not see them lit again in our lifetime.' He had just given in Parliament what a critic, Lord Hugh Cecil, described as a 'very wonderful' speech. Indeed, in Cecil's judgment it was, 'I think, in the circumstances, one may say the greatest speech delivered in our time or for a very long period … the greatest example of the art of persuasion that I have ever listened to.' This reminds us how unclear it was that politicians or the public would rally behind a war. It was only when the House cheered him that officials accepted that Grey had carried the day. Then the German Ultimatum and its rejection arrived, and he returned to the despatch box to inform the House. Next came that memorable comment, reported by G M Trevelyan in his biography, *Grey of Fallodon*. On the following day, Grey telegraphed the government's response, rejecting the German position and requiring a reply by midnight. There being no response, the country was at war.

The matter-of-fact way in which other Vincent's men went to war is illustrated by G D 'Khaki' Roberts, the rugby international and barrister. The fateful 3 August 1914 was the Bank Holiday Monday. Roberts was playing cricket in a match which was at so modest a standard that the village green did not have a pavilion. Sheltering from the rain under the trees, there was no prospect of play at tea-time, but every prospect of war, so Roberts tells us they abandoned the match with the understanding that, 'We will finish the game after the war' – although in the event half the players were killed in the conflict. The next morning, 4 August, Roberts enlisted in the Inns of Court Officers' Training Corps (Territorial Force) at Lincoln's Inn and, at about midnight, he was 'one of the crowd in front of Buckingham Palace, and we all cheered wildly to acclaim the preservation of our national honour'. It took exactly a year for training before Roberts arrived at the front at Festubert. He was one of the officers held back from the early stages of the Battle of Loos in case of heavy casualties. All his more senior officers were indeed killed in the early engagements, so he became the officer commanding, having never fought. He still did not have much to do, he modestly reports. He met 'many of my old rugger playmates' such as Hugh Martin who had some heavy artillery in front of him. Roberts told Martin he was 'behind the scrum as usual'. Roberts does not interrupt his wartime narrative to remind the reader that Hugh Martin is the only player in varsity history to have scored hat-tricks of tries in two games against Cambridge, and was the extraordinary winger whose four tries in the varsity match of 1909 would have been a record and received more recognition if the other winger, Ronnie Poulton, had not scored five tries. Poulton, who cross-kicked for one of Martin's tries and who also scored 'two cracking goals in the last eight minutes' of the 1909 varsity hockey match, is still holder, now jointly with Chris Ashton, of the record of four tries for England in an international (Poulton in the centre in England's last international before the War, v France, 1914; Ashton on the wing v Italy, 2011). By this stage, Ronnie Poulton had already been killed on his first day in the trenches.

Vincent's members of all ages and from all parts of the Empire were presenting themselves as volunteers, ready to fight. Some were too old and had to keep trying to find ways to make their contribution. Guy Nickalls, as we have seen, was determined to fight and did so in his 50s. By 1917, even the founder of Vincent's, W B Woodgate, in his 70s, had found a way to show his solidarity, volunteering to serve with the forerunner of the Home Guard. The president of the National Association of Volunteer Training Corps throughout the war was Vincent's William Grenfell, Lord Desborough, in his late 50s and early 60s. Like many Vincent's members, Grenfell lost sons in the war. Sir Edward Grey wrote movingly to Warden Pember, for example, on the death of the latter's son. Grey had sought to avert war but rose to the occasion when it became inevitable. If there was an oddity in his approach to his record-breaking stint as Foreign Secretary it is that, rather like the founder of Vincent's, he only once during those years went abroad. Of this older generation, Nickalls' fitness was most directly deployed. He returned from America, became a physical training instructor for the troops in France, then let his polo expertise and his field sports take him into action, recalling 'a tremendous aerial battle taking place overhead. I loosed off a rifle at three Fokkers, since they were quite close, and it seemed to help, for the Fokkers flew off'. He was looking for bottles of champagne a few days ahead of his birthday when he heard that there was to be an armistice. When he saw his name on a list recommended for an OBE, he put a pen through it because the 'government was far too free in giving honours to shirkers in England or at the bases, and very niggardly as regards the platoon commanders and Tommies'.

Vincent's men of younger years were just as swift to volunteer and just as modest about their contributions to the war effort. The last Vincent's president before the First World War, Captain David McLean Bain, died in the Battle of Festubert in 1915, where Roberts had first arrived. The president of 1909 and an Olympic gold medal-winner in 1912, Alister Kirby, died of illness while serving in the Rifle Brigade in France in 1917. Ronald Lagden, president in 1912, a South African Rhodes Scholar and quadruple Blue in rugby, cricket, hockey and rackets, died in between the first and second battles of Ypres on 3 March 1915. Commanding his company from the front, and at the front, he led 300 men over the top and was one of more than 100 who died. Tommy Nelson, president in 1899, has already been described in the last chapter by his friend Colonel John Buchan.

The most direct and immediate influence on Oxford sport of the Great War heroes came from those who fought, lived and returned to leadership roles in the student body. In particular, Major Ewart Horsfall MC DFC and Major Bevil Rudd MC made exceptional contributions before, during and after the Great War. Horsfall, one of those who won gold rowing in the Stockholm 1912 Olympics, and who in 1913 had become the first stroke of a Boat Race crew to win having been behind at Barnes Bridge, was awarded the Military Cross in 1916, then trained as a pilot and was awarded the Distinguished Flying Cross in 1918 before returning to Oxford and becoming president of Vincent's. He won silver in the eights at the Antwerp 1920 Olympics and was manager of Great Britain rowing in the London 1948 Olympics.

In 1913, the South African Bevil Rudd had won his first athletics Blue. Then he fought in the First World War. He returned to study, becoming president of the OUAC and of Vincent's, and winning a complete set of gold, silver and bronze at the Antwerp 1920 Olympics – gold in the 400, anchoring South Africa to silver in the 4 x 400 and gaining a bronze in the 800. This must be the quintessential

Vincent's presidential performance. Bevil Rudd went on to write well about athletics, principally for the *Daily Telegraph* and *Sunday Telegraph* but also as editor of the Achilles Club's book *Athletics* (1938 edition), in which he said that coaches should respect different styles of running – like a made-to-measure suit, not a straitjacket. Rudd was honorary secretary and later honorary chairman of Achilles between the Berlin and London Olympics. More than a decade after his death, one of the Cambridge athletes of his time, Philip Noel-Baker, himself an Olympic champion, was an MP being congratulated in the Commons on his Nobel Peace Prize. The debate was on Marshall scholarships. Noel-Baker did not dwell on his own honour but returned swiftly to the task before him, praising the value to international politics of promoting student opportunities abroad, and singling out 'Bevil Rudd, of South Africa, one of the most brilliant men who ever came out of that country and whose record for gallantry and resource in the First World War – in which he served in tanks – was equal to any'. The citation for Bevil Rudd's Military Cross reads:

> T./Lt. (A./Capt.) Bevil Gordon d'Urban Rudd, Tank Corps. For conspicuous gallantry and devotion to duty. He commanded six Tanks in action, and when the advance had been held up by heavy fire he pushed forward beyond the final objective, enabling the infantry to advance and hold the position. On the following day he drove the enemy several hundred yards further back, inflicting, heavy casualties. By his courage and skill he saved a critical situation.

Many heroes did not return from the war and some who did were no longer able or willing to pursue sporting achievement on the pitch, nor minded to commit further energies to leadership roles in student life. There are many Vincent's holders of the Military Cross and other awards, with two Vincent's men, Noel Chavasse and Geoffrey Woolley, winning the Victoria Cross in the First World War. The former died and his story is well known. The latter lived until the 1960s and is nowadays almost unknown. Chavasse was the only person to win the Victoria Cross twice (described as the Victoria Cross and bar) in the First World War. He also won the Military Cross. Woolley was the first Territorial Army officer to win the VC, and his bravery was also recognised on another occasion by the award of the Military Cross. Both were committed Christians. Chavasse was the son and twin brother of bishops and might have become a clergyman himself. He was serving as a medic and is a rare example not only of a double VC but of one who never fired a shot. Woolley was about to become an Anglican clergyman when war broke out and he did take Holy Orders after the War. Although his story and name are not so well known, the picture drawn in *The Illustrated London News*, depicting his actions in winning the VC, is a defining image of the battle at the front.

Noel Chavasse and his twin brother Christopher both ran the 440 yards (402 metres) for Great Britain in the London 1908 Olympics. Noel, a doctor, went with the Royal Army Medical Corps to Ypres where he won the Military Cross in June 1915 for almost two days of tending to the wounded. In July 1916 at Guillemont he repeated this heroism and was reckoned to have saved 20 seriously wounded men, as well as carrying one on a stretcher under heavy shelling for some 500 yards to safety. This merited the Victoria Cross. At the of July and the beginning of August 1917 he did it again north of Ypres, was injured in no man's land and died. A posthumous bar was awarded to his Victoria Cross (that is, a second award of the same standing as the initial Victoria Cross) for his 'extraordinary energy and inspiring example'. Lord Michael Ashcroft, who bought Chavasse's medals and has put them on display on loan to the Imperial War Museum, judges that Noel has the most memorials dedicated to him of any holder of the Victoria Cross. The medals had passed to St Peter's College, founded by Noel's brother, Christopher, who became the Bishop of Rochester. Initially St Peter's Society, it was founded in memory of their father, who was the Bishop of Liverpool when Noel died but who had been the rector of St Peter-le-Bailey in New Inn Hall Street, Oxford, when they were born, and then Principal of Wycliffe Hall. There were other brothers who fought in the war and sisters who supported the war effort. Christopher, his twin, and Bernard their younger brother also won the Military Cross, while Aidan was another one of the heroes who died at the front. Their father, Frank Chavasse, had not been expected to make his way in the world for three reasons: he was poor, had a stammer and was a hunchback. Within a generation, his modest and religious family had become famous for their heroism in war. Noel and Christopher had represented Oxford in athletics and lacrosse. It is easy nowadays to talk about sport in terms of heroics but almost a century ago Noel Chavasse's courage puts sport in perspective. He was a medic who never fired a shot, but was the most highly decorated hero of the war. Noel's first VC citation said that his courage and self-sacrifice were beyond praise. His second citation tells the story of his final days:

> Though severely wounded early in the action whilst carrying a wounded soldier to the dressing-station he refused to leave his post, and for two days not only continued to perform his duties but in addition went out repeatedly under heavy fire to search for and attend to the wounded who were lying out. During these searches, although practically without food during this period, worn with fatigue and faint with his wound, he assisted to carry in a number of badly wounded men over heavy and difficult ground. By his extraordinary energy and inspiring example he was instrumental in rescuing many wounded who would have otherwise undoubtedly succumbed under the bad weather conditions. This devoted and gallant officer subsequently died of his wounds.

Lieutenant Geoffrey Harold Woolley was one of two soldiers to win the VC in the fight for 'Hill 60', near Ypres, a contested height because it allowed those who held it to see for miles around. To take it from the Germans, mines were laid and exploded on Saturday, 17 April 1915, followed by heavy artillery shelling and then the infantry attack. All that worked, but could the Hill be held as thousands of German reinforcements marched to take back the crucial position? They had bayonets, bombs, shells filled with acid and hand-grenades.

Geoffrey Woolley of Queen's College had joined the Officers' Training Corps and volunteered to fight when war broke out, instead of proceeding to holy orders. Just as Kelly was bound to be described as giving too muscular an interpretation of Chopin at the keyboard, so Woolley was bound to be described as 'British and unassuming to the core, and a typical specimen of muscular Christianity. He excels at cricket, tennis, and football, and played the greater game of war with all his heart and soul'. This comes from the emotional account by G A Leask in *Heroes of the Great War* (1917). Woolley's regiment, the 9th Battalion London Regiment, was known as the Queen Victoria Rifles. By November 1914, they were ready for the front, near Ypres, where they were working in the trenches. 'On the very first day that he went into the trenches, Lieutenant Woolley showed his mettle. A hand-grenade was flung into his trench; without a moment's hesitation the young officer picked it up, and before the fuse had burned to the charge, flung it out. His prompt and plucky act saved not only his own life, but the lives of at least six or seven of his men.' On the night of 20–21 April 1915 the Germans attacked the trench held by Lieutenant Woolley's regiment. 'One by one Lieutenant Woolley's superior officers – a major, captain, and a lieutenant – had been killed.'

He organised counter-attacks and led his men in throwing bombs at the vastly superior force of the enemy. Standing on the parapet of the trench, fully exposed to the enemy, Woolley hurled bomb after bomb. His men urged him to seek shelter, but he refused. For some time this amazing contest continued, a handful of British against thousands of Germans. But this little band of heroes by their superb bravery, led by a hero, kept the enemy at bay. When welcome relief eventually came, the company of 150 men had been thinned to 20–14 Territorials and six Regulars, a pathetic proof of the dauntless fight put up by our men.

This was a pivotal battle for the war on the Western Front. Woolley suffered from gas poisoning and had a nervous breakdown.

His citation reads:

> For most conspicuous bravery on 'Hill 60' during the night of 20th–21st April, 1915. Although the only officer on the hill at the time, and with very few men, he successfully resisted all attacks on his trench, and continued throwing bombs and encouraging his men until relieved. His trench during all this time was being heavily shelled and bombed and was subjected to heavy machine gun fire by the enemy.

Two days later Woolley was promoted directly to the rank of Captain. He saw further action in the early stages of the Second Battle of Ypres until he was invalided back to England suffering from poison gas and psychological effects. When Woolley had recovered, he was appointed as an instructor at the Officers Infantry School. He returned to the Western Front in summer 1916. After the war, he taught at Rugby and was a chaplain at Harrow. In the Second World War, he became Senior Chaplain in Algiers in November 1942, reaching the rank of Chaplain to the Forces 3rd Class (Major). He died in 1968 having written in Vincent's centenary year, 1963, a memoir, *Sometimes a Soldier*.

Woolley's sporting career was not as distinguished as that of Chavasse, who himself was eliminated in his London 1908 Olympic heat, so it is appropriate to consider also what happened to a couple of members, as well as the Vincent's presidents noted above, who had already achieved greatness in sport. In F S Kelly and Arnold Strode Jackson, Vincent's has a 1908 Olympic gold medallist who was killed in action and a 1912 Olympic gold medallist who survived. A portrait of the latter holds a commanding position in the Club's premises. We left the former, the greatest of scullers, the Australian-born F S Kelly, in 1908 after his last race and his last word on how to scull. He had lived in Germany in pursuit of his career as a musician, a concert pianist and a composer. Some music critics found it difficult to forgive him for his sporting reputation. Kelly's diary entry on 18 October 1910 records, of the reviews of his performance, that: 'On the whole they were fairly just, but one critic said a thing which I foresee will be repeated wherever it is known that I was a sculler – i.e. my playing was perhaps a little too muscular for an interpretation of Chopin.' When war came, Kelly sailed to the Dardanelles with the Hood Battalion, becoming friendly with the Cambridge poet Rupert Brooke, who died from a mosquito bite on 23 April 1915. Kelly and friends buried him on the Greek island of Skyros. Kelly was wounded at Gallipoli. While recuperating, Kelly wrote his *Elegy for string orchestra* in memory of Brooke. Kelly returned to Gallipoli in July and was among the last soldiers to be evacuated off the Gallipoli Peninsula. He was awarded the Distinguished Service Cross for conspicuous gallantry at Gallipoli. The Hood Battalion went to France in May 1916. At the end of the last great Battle of the Somme, Kelly was killed on 13 November, age 35, while leading an attack against a machine-gun emplacement.

Kelly's elegy was first performed in Downing Street for the Prime Minister, Herbert Asquith. It is soft, evoking the wind whistling through Brooke's resting-place, a Greek, we could say Olympian, grove. When it was played again by the BBC for Armistice Day 2010, there was a lovely letter to *The Guardian* from Colin Clifford, Wednesday 17 November 2010:

> I was delighted by your editorial (In praise of … Frederick Septimus Kelly, 12 November) after Radio 3 played the Anglo-Australian composer's Elegy to his friend, Rupert Brooke, following the two-minute silence on Remembrance Day. At the time of Brooke's death, Kelly wrote: 'He is one of those, like Keats, Shelley and Schubert, who are not suffered to deliver their full message.' The same message applies even more to Kelly himself. Yet the music he did write deserves much greater recognition. He was a remarkable man: not just the best oarsman of his

generation and a talented, if unfulfilled, composer, but adored by his comrades in the Royal Naval Division. Universally known as 'Cleg', he kept everyone cheerful on his troopship in the days before the Gallipoli landings, hammering out popular music-hall songs and sea shanties on the ship's piano. In France the following year, he persuaded the high command to allow him to conduct the divisional band in a performance of Tchaikovsky's 1812 Overture to the accompaniment of a real artillery barrage.

All-round heroic service does not come much more rounded than that, winning and losing and winning again on the water, including Olympic gold, an Australian who lived in Germany, a composer and concert pianist who fought at Gallipoli and the Somme and was not above bashing out tunes on board ship or orchestrating the biggest of bangs for a famous overture on the battlefield. As Prime Minister David Cameron has promised a fitting commemoration and celebration of the heroism of the First World War, the centenaries of Kelly's wartime activities, and those of fellow Vincent's heroes, could serve many purposes. One hundred years on, there is already a revival of interest in Kelly's musical creativity.

What might have happened had Kelly and others lived is part of the incalculable human losses of war. Another of Vincent's gold medal winners lived for another 60 years although he too could have been killed at the Somme. The Olympic 1912 1500 metres champion, Arnold Jackson, was with the Rifle Brigade there when on 10 July 1916 they went over the top and 400 men were shot dead by machine guns. At Arras in April 1917, Jackson (by now a Major) was awarded a Distinguished Service Order and then a bar (a second award) within a few weeks. This citation explains that, 'Although wounded on two separate occasions [he] was able to carry out most valuable work. By his skill and courage he offered a splendid example to all ranks with him.'

Jackson fought all through the Third Battle of Ypres, also known as Passchendaele, and in March 1918 the citation for another bar to his DSO explained that,

It was entirely due to his powers of command and the splendid spirit with which he inspired his men that the attack on the greater part of his front was repulsed, and that the enemy, though they penetrated into parts of the front line, were counter-attacked and held at bay until the arrival of reinforcements. By his skilful dispositions he materially assisted the counter-attack which finally drove the enemy back with heavy losses and completely re-established the position.

Another bar was added later in 1918, again for his

conspicuous gallantry and brilliant leadership. During an attack by our troops Lt-Col Jackson advanced with the leading wave of his battalion, and was among the first to reach the railway embankment. The machine-gun fire against them was intense, but the gallant leading of this officer gave such impetus to the assault that the enemy's main line of resistance was broken.

He was subsequently wounded during the work of consolidation. He became, at 27, the youngest (acting) brigadier in the British Army. But a week before the end of the war, he was seriously wounded in the leg while fighting on the Belgium border, an injury which ended any thoughts of returning to competition on the track and left him with a limp. Off the track, he continued to offer advice, including back in Vincent's from its centenary year onwards, when he returned to England, after the death of his wife, for the last decade of his life. In between times he had participated in the Versailles peace treaty negotiations, for which he was awarded the CBE, emigrated to the United States, directed the first Kentucky Derby Festival, made a success of other business ventures and served as a Colonel on the staff of the Governor of Kentucky during the Second World War.

Some Vincent's members who fought in the First World War survived to return to Oxford, start work in other professions and even see action in the Second World War before resuming their high-flying careers. An Australian example is Sir Edmund 'Ned' Herring, who as a schoolboy in 1912 had played cricket in Australia for Ballarat against the visiting MCC side, which included Jack Hobbs. Ned scored a 50 and his brother a century. Jack Hobbs scored a century and a 50. In the summer of 1913, Ned Herring played for Oxford in the Parks against a Kent team that included Frank Woolley, who scored an unbeaten double century. Then Herring went to war, serving on the front in France and Macedonia. He won the Military Cross in 1917 on the Doiran front and was awarded the Distinguished Service Order at the end of the war. He became a member of

Vincent's on his return to Oxford. As he had already been awarded a law degree in the special circumstances of the war, he studied for the Bachelor of Civil Law degree. He led artillery brigades as a reservist between the wars while developing his practice back in Australia as a barrister, becoming a King's Counsel. He had been a Rhodes Scholar and had something of Cecil Rhodes' politics, standing as an independent right-wing candidate and participating in a secret society ready to fight, if necessary, to uphold the Empire and to quell any communist uprising.

In the Second World War, he led artillery brigades in North Africa in 1941 and was appointed CBE after victories over the Italians at Bardia and Tobruk. His deployment of artillery saved allied lives in the retreats in Greece, for which in 1942 he was awarded the Greek Military Cross. He then led the 6th Division in the Middle East before returning to defend Australia from attack by Japan. After the Japanese air raid on Darwin, he became commander of forces in the Northern Territory in 1942 and commanded the New Guinea Force and I Corps. This involved working with the Americans in the battle for beachheads in Papua New Guinea. He confirmed the death penalty on 22 local people who had handed over seven missionaries to the Japanese forces, who raped, tortured and killed their prisoners. The 22 collaborators were hanged publicly. When this became news 35 years later, Herring declared that his conscience was clear. In 1943 he was awarded the American Distinguished Service Cross and a knighthood for his service in Papua New Guinea. The brigadier next to him died when their plane crashed on take-off, but he survived. In 1944 he was appointed Chief Justice of Victoria and Lieutenant-Governor in 1945. By the centenary of Vincent's in 1963, he was still serving in those roles. He retired as Chief Justice in 1964 and as Lieutenant-Governor in 1972. Sir Edmund Herring died in 1982 and was given a state funeral.

Some of those who risked their lives serving as medics on the front line survived as heroes in both world wars. Hugh Kingsley Ward came to New College as the 1911 Rhodes Scholar for New South Wales. He rowed for Australia at the Stockholm 1912 Olympics. This was a controversial selection, criticised for breaking up the crew. Ward was part of the Australian squad but was at New College and rowed against the Australian crew at Henley, after which he was brought into the Australian boat, which did not make it to the final. He won Blues in the 1913 and 1914 Boat Races before volunteering for the Royal Army

Medical Corps Special Reserve on Wednesday 5 August 1914. Within a week, he was serving in France. A regimental medical officer, he became a captain and was wounded in action repeatedly, at Loos in 1915, the Somme in 1916 and Zeebrugge in 1917. He was left with no option but to surrender in July 1917 and be taken prisoner at Nieuport-Les-Bains in Belgium. In a handwritten note easily traceable on the internet, his explanation can be seen, that his officers were all dead or wounded and the only way to call for reinforcements was through sending messages by pigeon so 'I surrendered my wounded, my staff and stretcher-bearers, & no bombs were thrown into the dressing-station'. After eight months as a prisoner of war in Baden he returned to duty and was gassed at Arras in 1918 but continued to serve as a medic. He was awarded the Military Cross and two Bars, the first coming in 1916 for showing 'an utter contempt for danger' while attending to wounded men.

After the war, he returned to research in Oxford, then at Harvard University, back to Oxford and on to the Harvard staff. He encouraged John Enders to research infectious diseases, work for which Enders received a Nobel Prize. In 1935, Ward became a professor of bacteriology back at the University of Sydney, where he also chaired the Sports Union grounds committee from 1937 to 1951: the H K Ward sports gym was named after him. When in 2012, it was due for demolition, the works had to be delayed on safety grounds and the heroism of H K Ward was remembered: 'the HK Ward building seemed to heed the credo of the man after whom it is named and refused to go down without a fight.'

Just as H K Ward worked behind the scenes in Sydney to support subsequent generatons of students in their sporting ambitions, Senior Members of the University of Oxford had kept Vincent's open during the war and discreetly helped the new presidents, Horsfall and Rudd, in getting the Club and Oxford sport back on a sound footing. A prime example was J C Masterman, whose story stretches backwards and forwards to link Vincent's most famous members. J C Masterman had become a member of Vincent's in 1912, when he was expecting the president of OUAC, Anderson, to win gold at Stockholm. He was in Germany when the First World War broke out and was interned. In early 1919, he wrote in *The Times* about the revival of Oxford sport. In the inter-war years, he then lived up to this by his personal example as a scholar-athlete. In his autobiography, he recalls with pride that, 'I kept up most of my games until the outbreak of the Second World

War, and I confess that a newspaper cutting in January 1936 still gives me pleasure [he was writing in 1975 and he was 44 years old in 1936]:

> Few men can have played three different games in first-class company within a week … yet J C Masterman can claim that distinction during the past seven days. Last Tuesday he played in the South of England squash championship; over the weekend he was active on Rye golf course playing for the President's Putter; yesterday he scored two goals against the Cambridge hockey team.'

In those years, he also played hockey for England and competed in tennis at Wimbledon, partnered F E Smith in country house tennis doubles, worked as a don and emerged as a writer, with his first detective story, *An Oxford Tragedy*, published in 1927, being particularly well received. The fame of Oxford as an ideal setting for this genre owes much to Masterman. Before and after the First World War, he met Arthur Johnson.

Writing in the 1970s, Masterman comes across as a little unsporting in his reactions to that Vincent's member from the 1860s who had won the FA Cup a century before. He had not forgiven Johnson, who was in charge of the entrance scholarship examinations for 'Merton, University, and Brasenose Colleges' in April 1909, for dismissing Masterman and some other candidates after the first two days, without being allowed to take the remaining papers. Masterman regarded this 'execution' as an inexcusable 'act of cruelty'. He got his own back. He succeeded in the Worcester examinations and interviews in June, did well as an undergraduate and became a don. After the internment already mentioned, he returned to Oxford and met Johnson in 1919 as fellow examiners for entrance scholarships. Johnson drafted more than 30 questions, 'most of which seemed to [Masterman] to have done duty many times before'. Masterman carefully constructed his own questions but only three survived Johnson's critique. So Masterman sought support from his chief at Christ Church, Arthur Hassall, who played his part splendidly. He asked Masterman to identify his three questions, then attacked the draft paper in the examiners' meeting: 'This is a ridiculous paper, he said, there are only three decent questions on it.' 'And which are they?' was Arthur Johnson's unwise response. Hassall read out Masterman's three. Johnson was out-foxed and told Hassall: 'if you don't like the paper, go away and write a better one'. Hassall and Masterman did. The latter 'could not help feeling that my second clash with Arthur Johnson over scholarships amply avenged me for my earlier disaster'.

This petty squabble makes most FA Cup winners seem by comparison the mature ones. An Oxford graduate who went on to be a university lecturer elsewhere, Stephen Potter, coined the term Gamesmanship, based on some of the tactics of J C Masterman, a master gamesman. But Masterman's 1975 autobiography, *On the Chariot Wheel*, challenges the commonly held view that sport is a distraction from scholarship: 'I do *not* think that in schools and universities we pay too much attention to athletic success; I believe that games help the development of character and assist the growth of scholarship.' In Masterman's judgment, games 'breed a spirit of tolerance'. Indeed, 'no other activity promotes communication both between individuals and between countries' to such good effect, bringing people together. For Masterman, 'the majority of the friendships which I have made and such understanding as I have acquired of other people and other points of view stem from active participation in games'. Much of this socialising was in and through Vincent's.

Opinions might differ as to whether Masterman's understanding of other people is a good advertisement for the value of sport. It is difficult to know what is bluff and what is counter-bluff with Masterman, as befits someone who worked for MI5 in the Second World War. He was accepted despite, or perhaps because of, his interviewer remembering an acrimonious encounter on the hockey pitch. For MI5, he ran the 'double cross' system of spies during the war and published his book about it, after a long dispute with the government about the wisdom of explaining what had happened, in 1972. *The Double Cross System in the War of 1939–1945* records his experiences as Chair of the Twenty Committee during the Second World War, the Roman numerals for twenty being, of course, XX, a double cross. A year after Masterman, Whitney Shepardson, a Rhodes Scholar, had joined Vincent's in 1913. Shepardson too became a spymaster, rising to the higher echelons of the CIA. Airey Neave, after escaping from Colditz, used his expertise to help other prisoners make 'home runs', then carried out important roles at the Nuremberg war trials and remained close to the intelligence services throughout his rise as a Tory MP and shadow cabinet member to the eve of the 1979 general election, when republican terrorists killed him with a car bomb in the precincts of the Palace of Westminster. It is not far-fetched to suggest that some of the qualities of Vincent's men appealed to those recruiting spies and that Masterman would have been familiar with the officers of the Club over almost 50 years, from joining in 1912 to becoming Honorary treasurer of Vincent's and retiring as Provost of Worcester after serving from 1946 to 1961, including a two-year term as Vice-Chancellor 1958–59.

Horsfall, Rudd, Masterman and others had certainly revived Oxford sport. The 1920s and 1930s saw many heroics on tracks and fields, as well as on Woodgate's beloved water. After Rudd's extraordinary achievements at Antwerp 1920, other Vincent's Olympian successes included Alan Valentine winning rugby gold for the USA in Paris 1924, Crown Prince (later King) Olav winning sailing gold for Norway in Amsterdam 1928 and, on the track, Bill Stevenson winning 4x400 relay gold for the USA. 'Jumbo' Edwards won two golds in rowing at Los Angeles 1932 and Vincent's president Jack Lovelock won the 1500 metres, in front of Adolf Hitler, in a new world record at the 1936 Berlin Olympics.

The period was spanned by Arthur (later Sir Arthur and then Lord) Porritt of New Zealand. He was a Rhodes Scholar at Magdalen, a distinguished surgeon, doctor to the Queen and to her father, the first New Zealander to be Governor-General there, president of the OUAC and an Olympic medallist, taking bronze to Harold Abrahams' gold in the Paris 1924 100-metres immortalised in the Oscar-winning film, *Chariots of Fire,* to which he was an adviser (but in which he did not get the credit on the track as his performance was attributed to a Cambridge character for dramatic convenience). *The Independent* obituary gives a flavour of the person:

> President of the Oxford University Athletic Club in 1925–26; an athletics Blue in 1923–26, during which time he held the university's 100 yards and 220 yards hurdles records, and the 100 yards for Oxford v Cambridge with a time of 9.9 seconds. He captained the New Zealand Olympic team in Paris in 1924, where he won a bronze medal in the 100 metres, behind the British sprinter Harold Abrahams. His Olympic career continued as Captain at the Amsterdam Games in 1928, as Manager in Berlin in 1936 and for many years on the International Olympic Committee and British Olympic Council, and as Vice-President of the British Empire and Commonwealth Games Federation. Porritt's speed and scoring ability kept him in the vintage pre-war St Mary's rugby side during some of their best seasons. Porritt carried the athlete's directness and simplicity into his surgical work. With prophetic

foresight, and considerable professional courage, he went against the mainstream of surgical opinion in his treatment of two of the commonest conditions, hernia and cancer of the breast … Arthur Porritt was also an army surgeon of renown [in] war service with the 21st Army Group in North Africa and Europe … In the 1960s he was President of the Royal College of Surgeons of England and then returned home as the first New Zealand-born Governor-General. He was made a life peer in 1973.

Jack Lovelock was an inspiration to the post-war generation of Sir Roger Bannister and many others. Porritt, Lovelock, Bannister and other Oxford athletes formed bonds with Cambridge opponents, not least through the Achilles Club. One of the most moving illustrations of all this necessarily brings a great Cambridge man into this story. Harold Abrahams was a gold medallist of distinction, an administrator and selector, and a commentator. As a well-known Jewish sportsman, he was in favour of not boycotting Hitler's Olympics but of supporting those who challenged the Nazis. As the great Cambridge and British Olympian, he was so supportive of the Oxford New Zealander that he completely lost that BBC impartiality as Lovelock rounded the final bend:

> Lovelock leads by about four yards. Cunningham fighting hard, Beccali coming up to his shoulder, Lovelock leads … Lovelock … Lovelock … Cunningham second, Beccali third … Come on, Jack! One hundred yards to go … Come on, Jack! By God he's done it! Jack, come on! Lovelock wins! Five yards, six yards, he wins … he's won! Hooray!'

Lovelock's pace was so quick that Vincent's Jerry Cornes' personal best, lowering his 1932 silver time, only placed him sixth, with the first five all beating the Olympic record. Guy Walters' enthralling account of the Berlin Games reports also Lovelock's more measured diary entry that night: 'It was undoubtedly the most beautifully executed race of my career … a true climax to 8 years steady work, an artistic creation … Later felt a little weary but v fit.' In that book *Athletics*, edited by Rudd, Lovelock advises that 'knowledge of the pace both of oneself and of one's opponents is necessary to get the utmost from oneself, to prevent opponents from doing their best, and to raise middle distance running into the realms of a mental rather than a physical combat', lessons applied to war by that Vincent's spymaster,

J C Masterman, who turned being trapped in Germany when the First World War broke out (and almost again in 1939) into a strength, as he knew the opponents well enough to orchestrate that double cross system.

Vincent's Olympians were not above participating in college sport. Olav V and Harald V of Norway are the only Oxford-educated father and son kings to have competed in the Olympics. They were both students at Balliol. The Balliol Boat Club claims them both as having rowed for the College and news film footage exists of King Olav rowing at five in the Balliol third boat in Torpids, 1925. To the wider world, that might not count as much as King Olav's gold medal in sailing in the Amsterdam 1928 Olympics, or King Harald's gold medal in sailing's world championship in 1987, but to those who understand the spirit of Oxford sport it is a tribute fit for a king to say of any students that they turned out for their College at a humbler level in another sport.

Beyond the Olympics, the 1920s saw heroics in mountaineering. Sandy Irvine of Vincent's might, with George Mallory of Cambridge, have been the first to reach the top of Everest. Between 1914 and 1936, Oxford won the Boat Race only once, in 1923, by three-quarters of a length. One of the victorious Oxford crew was Andrew Comyn (known as 'Sandy') Irvine, who had also rowed the previous year. In June 1924, he died with Mallory, the country's most experienced mountaineer, close to the summit of Everest. It was unclear whether they were on their way up or down. Seventy-five years later, Mallory's body was found by one of the many attempts to retrieve the two corpses. The search continues to find Sandy Irvine's body. Irvine was chosen for the second Oxford University expedition to Spitzbergen as a direct result of his reputation for strength in the Boat Race. This Arctic adventure then led to his controversial selection for the Everest expedition even though he was an inexperienced climber, as his niece Julie Summers records in *Fearless on Everest – the Quest for Sandy Irvine* (2000), 'He was elected to the Oxford University Mountaineering Club and the president, in a rather droll obituary, wrote: "I never climbed with him; in fact, the only climb I ever saw him do was from a box at the Winter Gardens Theatre onto the stage".' Mallory had wanted him on the team, nonetheless, because, as he wrote to a friend, 'Irvine represents our attempt to get one superman, though lack of experience counts against him'. The 1999 Mallory & Irvine Research Expedition team concluded their book *Ghosts of Everest* in a telling fashion:

the story of Mallory and Irvine has captured the public imagination not simply because it is a good mystery but because it has meaning – and a different meaning – for each of us. Each of these individual 'stories' is a mix of fact and personal philosophy – about achievement and failure, about free will and fate, about mortality and immortality. In the end, the answer to the question 'Did they make it?' may well be another question: 'Does it matter?'. Surely what matters, what warrants our attention and our awe, is the scale of their achievement given the resources available to them, their astonishing strength and grit, the indomitability of their desire.

A high point in wider University life towards the end of the 1920s came when Sir Edward, now Lord, Grey was installed in the Sheldonian Theatre. Dr Cyril Baily of Balliol records a performance to trump even the legendary speeches of Harold Macmillan, who would often seem to be too frail to command an occasion before rallying to mesmerise those listening. According to Baily, Lord Grey

> asked me to write his Latin speech for him, giving me in English what he wanted to say. He was by that time very blind and it would have been impossible for him to read it. So he suggested that I should read it for him. A little later he wrote to me 'I have been looking at your speech and the roll of a Latin sentence is coming back to me. I might learn it by heart.' I shall never forget the magnificent dignity of his walk up the floor of the Sheldonian to his seat. When it came to the speech he delivered it just as if he were Cicero making it up as he went along, and there was never the faintest need for a prompt. When we met in the evening at the Balliol Gaudy he said to me 'I hear I used some words that were different from what you printed, and Pember said that mine were better,' and then went off into one of his glorious chuckles.

His old friend Francis Pember was Vice-Chancellor. Grey did not confine himself to ceremony or sport but followed three causes in particular, the Bodleian building schemes, the Oxford Preservation Trust and the creation of the Oxford Society. 'Having regard to his grave physical disabilities,' Herbert Fisher, Warden of New College declared, 'the measure of help which he was able to render in each of these three spheres of activity was a striking triumph of the character over the tribulations of the flesh.'

Spanning the 1920s and 1930s, an extraordinary character who triumphed over setbacks was Hugh 'Jumbo' Edwards. Richard Burnell, who went on to win gold himself at London 1948, wrote of Edwards, a Squadron Leader in the RAF when war broke out, that he

> was awarded the AFC in 1943 in recognition of his feat of airmanship in bringing home a badly damaged Hampden from one of the thousand bomber raids on Cologne, and the DFC in 1944. While commanding a squadron of Liberators on convoy escort duty he suffered the loss of three engines but successfully brought his aircraft down in the sea off the Cornish coast and escaped by sculling his rubber dinghy into the shipping lanes.

Edwards retired from the RAF as Group Captain in 1956. The reason Burnell was writing about him, however, is that this high-flyer was also a famous oarsman. He collapsed in the Boat Race in 1926 and took some years out to come to terms with this disappointment. He returned to row in another losing crew in the 1930 Boat Race but won at Henley the Grand Challenge Cup in the same year, and then in 1931 won three Henley finals in one day before winning two golds in a single day at the Los Angeles 1932 Olympics. He had been selected with another Christ Church rower, Lewis Clive, in the coxless pairs but also stepped into the coxless four, when a rower was ill.

Edwards went on to coach Oxford almost every year of the 1950s and 1960s, and the GB eight, an all-Oxford crew, for the Rome 1960 Olympics. He was fascinated by the technology of rowing, as Woodgate had been, and by the need for measuring and improving fitness, introducing ergometers. Like Woolley's recollections, his memoirs were published in Vincent's centenary year of 1963, entitled *The Way of a Man with a Blade*. This book shows that Edwards had taken some comfort after his 1926 collapse from the comment by Steve Fairbairn, the man who had praised Woodgate so fulsomely, that it was honourable to have rowed yourself to a standstill. An X-ray showed Jumbo had a dilated heart. In his own words, he was

> not asked to row in the Christ Church summer eight, which was Head of the River, although I was invited to do a little coaching of other college crews … I was then

rusticated for failing Pass Mods ... I was very angry at my complete failure both on the river and academically, but my resentment was directed, not against myself, but against those in authority ... against the college authorities who had terminated my studies. When I departed out of that city I shook the dust off my feet.

He came back only to get his RAF commission but then hardly left the water on Oxford's behalf after that other than to fly. By the end, the 1959 mini-mutiny questioned whether he was still right in his coaching methods, but he began that era with the big question of rowing style and at the great venue of the Club:

When I was one of the coaches for the 1949 Oxford crew, we had several conferences to thrash out details. I remember at one of these, held at Vincent's, I inquired what style we were going to teach.

Back in the 1930s, Jock Lewes became president of the Oxford University Boat Club before he, too, went on, like Jumbo Edwards, to be a war hero, also airborne. Lewes was brought up in Bowral, where Don Bradman and P L Travis, the author of *Mary Poppins*, also lived, about an hour outside Sydney. His family had a motto, 'as wise as a serpent, as gentle as a dove', the same expression as at W B Woodgate's Radley. Jock's father, Arthur, had studied at Christ Church and had met Charles Dodgson (who famously wrote as Lewis Carroll), Dean Liddell, and one of the Dean's daughters, Alice (after whom and for whom the *Alice* stories were written by Carroll). The father, who was often working away in the Middle East, wrote fantasy and adventure stories for his own children. The boys experimented with chemicals to make explosives. Jock Lewes' general essay paper for his Oxford entrance examination in 1933 included the question 'What new methods of warfare are likely to be adopted in the event of another war?'. Jock Lewes went on to invent the Lewes Bomb and to be the co-founder of the SAS, the Special Air Service, which in turn spawned many such special forces around the world, fighting traditional wars (and now terrorism) in unconventional ways. He won a Blue in the 1936 Boat Race and dropped himself as president from the 1937 crew, preferring to plot tactics and secure a remarkable victory. Like C B Fry, he was attracted to the blossoming of German pride before he understood the horrors of the Nazi regime, at which point he threw his considerable energies and ingenuity into defeating Nazi Germany and its Allies. A parachutist, he was killed on the SAS's second operation but he had already set out the basis of British and other special forces.

In cricket, the nearest equivalent as a sporting hero to Jumbo Edwards when the 1920s gave way to the 1930s was the Nawab of Pataudi. Scoring a century in his first varsity match in 1929, he scored a double century in 1931. A Cambridge batsman had also scored a double century and set a new varsity match record in their innings, but Pataudi overtook it and was 238 not out, which remained the highest score for over 70 years. He was one of Wisden's cricketers of the year in 1932. Pataudi eventually captained India after the Second World War but initially played for England, again scoring a century on his debut but having a disagreement of opinion with his captain, Vincent's Douglas Jardine, over the deployment of bodyline tactics in that 1932–33 Test series in Australia. Jardine – who was a more cavalier player than his reputation as the captain in that controversial way of restricting Donald Bradman allows – is said to have dismissed Pataudi as a 'conscientious objector'.

Pataudi, who was also a hockey Blue, died of a heart attack while playing polo. Jardine's father, another Vincent's man, had scored 140 in the varsity match of 1892 and Jardine was often accused of having a grudge against Australians as he was left on 96 not out when playing for Oxford against them in 1921. It is more likely the case that he simply decided that bowling short-pitched fast deliveries on the leg-side, with fielders there, was the best way of containing the world's greatest-ever batsman, Donald Bradman, a strategy that worked. Jardine himself stood up to similar tactics from the West Indies in 1933, scoring a century. Neville Cardus's verdict was that Jardine

> was a tall hard-boned personality, having none of the unction often associated in his period with cricket. His was a realpolitik. He determined in the early 1930s to wrest back the 'ashes' from Australia, and to put Bradman in a reasonable, if still high, place. All the howls and winds of the world would not deter him. As a batsman he was upright and unbending, strong in defence and to the onside. His hat was scrupulously straight. The fastest bowling could not hurry him. His batting, indeed, was like the man himself – calm, well bred, not given to rhetoric, common-sensed, and imperturbable. He had, off the field, a canny wit and gifts

for fellowship. On the field, even a Harlequin cap did not lighten or brighten his pervading air of relentless purpose. Against Australia he played cricket to win. He was perhaps the first to lead the reaction against Edwardian gesture and romance and the humbug of 'may the best side win'.

In stark contrast, rugby was soon to witness one of the most romantic of sporting legends, and one of the greatest sporting cavaliers. Oxford's Prince Alexander Obolensky's brief rugby union career had at least four sublime moments in a golden spell of less than two months at the end of 1935 and the beginning of 1936: one tackle against Cambridge in the middle of three tries against the All Blacks.

Obolensky was born in Russia but his family fled to England when he was a little child. As a student, he liked the high life of oysters, champagne and girl friends in London but also reviewed drama for *Isis* and wrote an essay in a book on religion, edited by Keith Briant and George Joseph in 1936, called *Be Still and Know: Oxford in Search of God*. He wrote of his unorthodox Orthodox belief in God that, 'what has been good for ten centuries of Obolenskys is still good enough for me'. Obolensky volunteered to become a pilot in the Royal Air Force and died in the early weeks of the war, in a training accident in East Anglia. There is now a statue of him in Ipswich, funded by admirers of his genius, including Roman Abramovich, but most of our memories come from one of the most famous tries in history, much celebrated at the Twickenham rugby museum. Prince Alexander was a cousin of a distinguished Oxford academic, Professor Sir Dimitri Obolensky, whose knowledge of Russian literature was itself legendary. Alexander, a schoolboy sprinter, was obsessive about something else altogether – lightweight boots. David Frost's magisterial history of varsity rugby records that Obolensky 'used to have coffee most mornings at Elmer Cotton's sports shop in The Turl, demanding ever-lighter and thinner boots. The Cotton family did their best to meet these demands, but Obolensky's boots were often so delicately made that they would split in the course of a match'.'

The famous tackle came at Twickenham in the varsity match of 10 December 1935, which fell between Obolensky's two games against the All Blacks. This had the unusual result of a 0-0 draw, not repeated since, but the nearest to a try came when the Cambridge wing, John Rawlence, was put clear by the centre Wilf Wooller. Tearing across from the opposite wing, Obolensky tackled Rawlence into touch. Wooller and many other fine judges regarded it as one of the greatest tackles of all time.

On 6 November 1935, Obolensky had scored an outstanding try for Oxford against New Zealand when the University just missed becoming the first team to beat the All Blacks in England, losing 9-10 at Iffley Road. In the international game itself at Twickenham, on 4 January 1936, he began by scoring a similar try, also of the highest quality, before the one that has become immortal. Both these tries against the All Blacks, the best team in the world, by the 19-year-old student had involved the classic winger's run round the defence to the corner. In this context, the genius of the most famous try which was so remarkable for his cutting inside becomes more apparent. Having twice rounded the All Blacks on the outside to score in the corner, first for Oxford, then for England, no wonder that he wrong-footed the defence when this time he scythed through the middle. England won 13-0, the first time the All Blacks had been defeated in England. Plaudits in the press included the comment that,

> His double swerve to gain his first try was remarkable enough, but the extraordinary turn-in and diagonal right-to-left run which won him his second and which drew forth that great Twickenham rarity, a double roar of applause, will never be forgotten by anybody who saw it.

The most succinct account was that Obolensky's unorthodoxy was 'a stupendous exhibition of the hypotenuse in rugby.'

Obolensky is reputed to have scored 17 tries in a single game v Brazil later that summer, in a warm-up game before the main Argentina section of the tour, but research so far, including scrutiny of newspaper coverage in the Twickenham museum archives, has yet to prove that this legend is true and all the indications are that it is not. What is attested is the legendary answer by Prince Alexander Obolensky that put the Prince of Wales, a fellow Vincent's member, in his place when the teams were being introduced to him before that famous match at Twickenham against New Zealand. There had been much controversy over whether Obolensky, who was in the process of becoming a naturalised citizen of this country, should have been selected. The Prince of Wales asked him, 'By what right do you play for England ?' Obolensky replied 'I attend Oxford University …

Sir'. Obolensky was dropped by England after four games. Nor did the Prince of Wales last long as King Edward VIII.

Obolensky's inside centre for Oxford, Micky Walford, was one of Vincent's most extraordinary all-round sportsmen and another war hero, who received the Military Cross. He won Blues for rugby, cricket and hockey, set up Obolensky for his first try against New Zealand, played cricket for Somerset and won silver in London 1948 at hockey for Great Britain. He played more than 150 times for the University across the three sports, thought to be a record. In rugby, he was the centre who passed to Obolensky when the Prince first scored against the All Blacks for Oxford, in November 1935. In the *Daily Telegraph*, Howard Marshall's account of the try for Oxford against the All Blacks was this: 'What a try it was ... out to ... Walford, who ran beautifully before he passed to Obolensky ....' E W Swanton's report was even more evocative: 'Oxford, with three-quarters of the game gone, were only a point behind. Micky Walford makes a sudden break from his own half and feeds the blond figure outside ....' Simon Wilkinson, in speaking at a thanksgiving service in Sherborne for the life of Micky Walford said of this that Swanton's 'reference to Micky was typical [of Walford] – inventive, imaginative, seeing the opening and generously making way for others'. He was 'as quick on his feet as a whippet', even in 1948 when he won silver with Great Britain hockey. Wilkinson says: 'After the match he was seen furtively leaving the ground clutching a cricket bag furtively. He had to; he was playing cricket for Somerset the next day.' In 1938, for Oxford against a MCC side at Lord's, when the University had needed a brisk approach in the final innings of the match, Walford scored 201* in 150 minutes and Oxford scored 280 for 1 to win the game.

That year, 1938, was the halfway point in Vincent's history. Wisden compiled a century of the greatest matches of the 20th century. The selection for 1938 was Western Province v Eastern Province. A Vincent's president, and yet another boxer, Pieter van der Bijl was left with the challenge of scoring 26 off the last over, admittedly an eight-ball over. He went for a six-ball finish, 446644. The following year, a more typical innings of his was that in the Timeless Test in Durban, where he took 45 minutes to get off the mark. His fellow opener and captain, Alan Melville, was also a Vincent's member. Van der Bijl scored 125, Melville 78. In the second innings, Melville, who was injured, dropped down the order but scored a century himself, 103. Van der Bijl opened with Mitchell who was out hit wicket for 89. Van der Bijl was a boundary away from a second century in the match when he hit a poor ball to a fielder and was out for 97. Despite being heralded as a Timeless Test, the match was abandoned as a draw on 14 March 1939, having started on 3 March. In *Cricketers of the Veld*, Louis Duffus described van der Bijl's first innings in heroic terms:

> Van der Bijl is a boxing Blue. He designed his innings as he might a heavyweight fight. In the first round – the morning – he was forced into a corner and took untold punishment. He became the fast bowlers' punching bag ... he was smitten hip and thigh without flinching. He played with a blind, stubborn courage.

Van der Bijl became a teacher, master in charge of cricket and then in charge of the whole prep shool at Bishops in Cape Town. One of his pupils, Clive van Ryneveld, became a double Blue and international in cricket and rugby after the War. He has written of his teacher's inspiration and explains that van der Bijl fought in the Second World War. But even he does not tell us that van der Bijl, like Rudd, won the Military Cross. The recommendation from Maj-Gen D H Pienaar in 1943 stated that,

> Captain van der Bijl has served with this Battalion with great distinction throughout. An armoured car platoon commander, he daily went out on patrol and at all times under fire showed leadership and courage of the very highest order. Whenever any dangerous job was to be done, Capt van der Bijl begged to be allowed to tackle it and his complete disregard for his personal safety and consideration for others was an inspiration to his men who would follow him anywhere. Not content with his daily patrol work he went out at night to reconnoitre enemy positions so as to be able to direct his daily patrols more effectively. On another occasion he volunteered for, and carried out, a dangerous mission behind enemy lines at Gazala. In enemy country and immediately in front of enemy lines Capt van der Bilj lay up for two days watching and studying enemy dispositions, under exhausting conditions, returning with valuable information. This officer has been one of the greatest sources of inspiration in the Battalion. His great cheerfulness under any conditions and his outstanding devotion to duty has been an example of inestimable value to all ranks.

Those values, virtues of Vincent's, are indeed timeless. They were illustrated time and again in the Second World War. Marmaduke Hussey played in a wartime cricket match and was selected for wartime rugby v Cambridge. There are disputes, which did not bother Hussey, as to whether these count as Blues. He was a member of Vincent's. Hussey had a broken bone in his hand and had been commissioned to fight in the war, so he pulled out of the varsity match to focus on being fit to fight. After winning medals for bravery, he was captured and had a leg amputated by German doctors in an Italian prison camp. That didn't stop him escaping and making it back to Vincent's. The Radcliffe Infirmary nurse said he would die if he didn't get his lower back treated properly. He asked if she'd heard of a doctor called Girdleston. She said he was the one person who could save Hussey's life. That was good news because Hussey had met him at the bar at Vincent's. He operated, Hussey survived and even survived being managing director of *The Times* and then Chairman of the BBC – hazardous jobs. He was knighted and then, 50 years after that encounter in Vincent's, Hussey was ennobled, living altogether for 60 years after meeting one of the country's leading surgeons over lunch in the Club.

On returning to Trinity after the war, Hussey had met at least four fellow Vincent's men in Trinity alone:

> seasoned war heroes like Dick Wakeford VC, Tommy Macpherson with three Military Crosses, and Ozzie Newton Thompson, a distinguished South African who captained Oxford at rugby and was awarded the Distinguished Flying Cross. Many of them had stunning careers at Oxford, not least Anthony Rowe, a musician and a scholar who had used sherry for ballast in his wartime submarine 'to cheer up the troops'. He captained the Oxford boat and won the Diamond Sculls. A genuine eccentric. It was a very larky place.

Rowe was one of three officers who took the Japanese surrender in Hong Kong in 1945. His obituary in the *Telegraph* has a telling phrase: 'After the war Philip Landon, the bursar of Trinity College, Oxford, sprung Rowe from the Navy by offering him a scholarship just in time for him to row in the 1946 Summer Eights. Trinity stayed Head by a whisker, and Rowe became Captain of Trinity College Boat Club for the next two years.' Landon was the Senior Member of Vincent's. Another Trinity undergraduate of this post-war era, Robin Fletcher, became Honorary treasurer of the Club, Bursar of Trinity and Warden of Rhodes House, winning a bronze medal for Great Britain in hockey at the Helsinki 1952 Olympics. Rowe reached the semi-final of the London 1948 Olympics as a single sculler, won the Stewards' at Henley in 1949, was president of Oxford University Boat Club, losing 'the Boat Race by six feet, a defeat he attributed to the goose and oyster pre-race dinner', won the Diamond Sculls at Henley in 1950, coached the Oxford crew in the mid-50s and then at the end of Vincent's first century in 1963, by which time he was running the only one of Penguin's printing firms that was bold enough to print the uncut *Lady Chatterley's Lover* which became a symbol of the 1960s. He took up riding at retirement age and rode across Africa, India and the Andes.

Sir Tommy Macpherson won the Military Cross three times, three *Croix de guerre*, a *Legion d'honneur* and a Papal knighthood, but in his autobiography it is clear how important Oxford sport was to him and that he appreciated being 'elected to the prestigious and largely sporting elite of Vincent's Club – with its famous dark-blue tie and the crowns upon it', not least because 'we sometimes dined in the club' as it was 'so affordable that it was no strain on the budget'. He had 'fought in Syria and North Africa, escaped from two of the most feared prisoner-of-war camps in Europe and orchestrated guerrilla operations in Italy and France', parachuting back into the fray, behind enemy lines, and on one occasion bluffing 23,000 soldiers of the SS Das Reich tank column into surrendering to him. But the only thing which is described in the book as causing him 'intense annoyance' is not getting his rugby Blue because the selectors would insist on choosing that gifted all-rounder Martin Donnelly at fly-half. Macpherson would have played himself at fly-half with Donnelly at centre. The England selectors chose Donnelly in that position for one unhappy game. In sport, Sir Tommy perhaps suffered because he himself writes that the greatest rugby player he ever saw was his older brother, G P S 'Phil' Macpherson, a Blue and Scottish international. In the introduction to *Behind Enemy Lines* in 2010, once he had turned 90, however, he explains that, while his sleep was blighted for years by memories of the war that he had wanted to forget, he now thought that survivors have something of a 'duty to remind the next generation of what war really entails'.

Through the war years, Philip Landon of Trinity was the don and Honorary treasurer who chaired committee meetings and ensured that club premises were kept as open as possible. There were still problems such as the theft of the clock and barometer from the Club Room and the pressing matter of selling the Club wines. Major J C Masterman was an assiduous attender, despite himself chairing the XX Committee in London which was more directly related to the war effort. By May 1945, a general meeting of the Club decided to offer 'congratulations to Major D H Macindoe on his being awarded the Military Cross'. In January 1946, the treasurer announced that there being 'no other proposals, Mr D H Macindoe was elected president of the Club *nem con*'. David Macindoe duly resumed playing cricket for Oxford, then returned to his old school, Eton, wrote a brilliant book on cricket in conversation with his predecessor at Eton, Claude Taylor, and oversaw cricket there until the end of the 1950s, becoming Vice-Provost of Eton.

Meanwhile, across the Atlantic as the war was ending, *Time* reported that Vincent's 'Rocket Man' had a new job: 'After six months of sifting through 150 candidates, Purdue University last week picked the nation's expert of experts on rocket bombs as its new president.' Fred Hovde was a former American Football star who played rugby for Oxford and became a research scientist. His daughter, in a book primarily about her own business career, recalls that, 'My dad delivered the message to Churchill that we were going to drop the atomic bomb' as he was Chief of Rocket Ordinance Research of the National Research Defence Committee and was sent to London to liaise on this. When he retired from Purdue in 1971, president Richard Nixon came to speak in praise of him:

> I knew, too, of his service in World War II in the most secret projects against the Nazis, service that perhaps could not even now be talked of in declassified terms because it was of such a highly important nature, and service that only a man with his background was able to perform. Only a very few were chosen, and because of what they did, the war was made shorter and victory came sooner, and he was one who helped ... [But] the Nation will remember him for the monument that he really leaves, and that monument is 80,000 men and women. Eighty thousand men and women have graduated from Purdue in the 25 years he has served as president.

Before the war, Roger Kimpton, an Australian, had scored a century against Gloucestershire in his second game for Oxford, won the freshmen's singles in tennis and had become a golf Blue. He scored centuries freely. Wisden thought he should curb his rashness but Kimpton became a fighter pilot in the Royal Australian Air Force, flying 140 sorties. His DFC citation says that 'by his aggressive and determined leadership [he] proved an inspiration to the pilots under his command'. After the war, Kimpton went into business.

Similarly, Vincent's Victoria Cross hero in the Second World War just got on with his studies and his profession, the law, afterwards without making a fuss about sport or his war service. Captain Richard Wakeford was awarded the VC for his courage when in command of the company which was leading the attack on the two hills near Monte Cassino, Italy, on 13 May 1944. The citation explains that

> Armed with a revolver, and accompanied by his orderly, he killed several of the enemy, taking 20 prisoners. The final objective, a house vigorously defended by a German officer and five men, was attacked by Captain Wakeford, who was driven back twice by grenades, before he managed to make a final run to reach the window, through which he was able to throw his grenades. Some of the enemy were killed and wounded, the remainder surrendered. The following day, after the initial surprise had been lost, a tank having become bogged down, they came under extremely heavy fire from the enemy which caused many casualties. Although wounded in both arms and the face, Captain Wakeford crossed the start line, leading his men forward. On the way up the Hill they came under heavy fire from Spandau guns. Despite his wounds he led an attack and dealt with the opposition. His company now came under heavy mortar fire and he was again wounded in the legs, but he carried on until he reached and consolidated his objective.

Of the war heroes who did come back to study and to play sport, the New Zealander Martin Donnelly was one who became known around the sporting world. Donnelly was a tank commander in Egypt during the war. He was released to play in exhibition matches at the end of the war in 1945, scoring three centuries in that year, one of which was in what Denzil Batchelor dubbed the perfect game, when the Dominions beat England at Lord's. In 1946, he scored six centuries, including a 142 against Cambridge. In 1947, he scored 162 for the Gentlemen against the Players and became, alongside fellow Vincent's man, Alan Melville, one of Wisden's Cricketers of the Year, where he was lauded as the world's best left-hander. In 1949, he scored a double century for New Zealand against England. In other tags, he was called the left-handed Bradman but Donnelly did not think that cricket was the be-all and end-all of life. He sailed to Australia, worked for Courtaulds and took up fly-fishing. The citation for Martin Donnelly in the New Zealand Sports Hall of Fame states: 'They said he had everything as a Test batsman: style and grace; confidence and determination; success and modesty'.

Of those who were schoolboys during the war, Clive van Ryneveld is an outstanding illustration of the talent in Vincent's in the late 1940s. He followed his brother's example, Tony, as a Rhodes Scholar, Vincent's member and rugby Blue. Clive went on to captain Oxford and South Africa at cricket and play rugby for England, as well as being there when Harold Macmillan came to Cape Town to give his famous 'wind of change' speech in 1960. Clive van Ryneveld had become a Progressive MP. A batsman who took seven wickets in one Cambridge innings at Lord's with his leg-breaks, he toured with the Greyhounds and met Pope Pius XII, when Tommy Macpherson was interpreter. He was surprised by food rationing in England and welcomed the meals at Vincent's. Clive van Ryneveld was one of those Vincent's Blues and internationals who would happily play Cuppers rugby, in his case winning with Univ. He was secretary of the Club when Roger Bannister was president.

In such company, a talented cricketer and Vincent's member in the post-war glory days of Oxford sport, Robert Hawke, struggled in the 1950s to get beyond duties as twelfth man for the varsity side. Even one of the stars of the team, Jimmy Allan, might not have expected anyone to have heard of him by comparison to Vincent's members Kardar, Melville, van Ryneveld, Cowdrey, and M J K Smith all of whom went on to captain their countries in the 1960s and 1970s, as did the Nawab of Pataudi (junior, sometimes known as Pat, sometimes as Tiger), by which time A C Smith was running Warwickshire and then the English Test & County Cricket Board, having like M J K Smith (no relation) captained Oxford for two years. A C Smith, also a soccer Blue, is a rare example of a wicket-keeper who took off his pads in first-class cricket and took a hat-trick. Even more unusually, he bowled off the wrong foot.

Colin Cowdrey has written various memoirs. In one, *MCC – The Autobiography of a Cricketer*, he recounts that in his three years playing for Oxford (without winning in the varsity match),

It was a delightful routine: breakfast, nets, the match, a beer or two, dinner at Vincent's and few cares. Vincent's Club was the haven for University sportsmen, a warm comfortable place, with its deep leather armchairs, polished wood, tankards of ale, and laughter. Meals were so reasonably priced that you could take in a visiting county player as a guest and do him proud with a good dinner for under a pound. What an evening of celebration it was when Roger Bannister, skilfully paced by Chris Chataway, broke the four-minute mile along the track at Iffley Road!

He played college football and squash for Brasenose and was first string in University Rackets in his first Hilary term, just before his Preliminary Examination in Geography. Colin Cowdrey played cricket for England for over 20 years, the first to play 100 Tests, captained them intermittently, scored over 100 first-class centuries (one in the varsity match in 1953) and over 20 in Tests. He was knighted and ennobled for services to cricket and became president of MCC, the club whose initials it had pleased his parents to give him in the expectation, when he was born in India, that he might one day play for them. One day in Australia he scored a triple century for the MCC. His gravestone epitaph was written in *The Times* by John Woodcock, 'some journey, some life, some cover drive, some friend'.

Woodcock himself won a hockey Blue and is another Vincent's member from the post-war era, one of the doyens of sportswriting, having for many years graced the pages of *The Times* as cricket correspondent. When M J K Smith retired from playing, Woodcock wrote:

By the time he went down from Oxford he had scored 201 not out in the University Match of 1954, followed by 104 in 1955 and 117 in 1956 when he was captain, a record that has never been equalled. He had been President of Vincent's Club too, an exclusive sporting establishment which is very careful about whom to have as its head; and he had played stand-off half for England ... Between 1957 and 1962 he never got fewer than 2125 runs in an English season; in 1959 he made 3245, including 166 for Gentlemen against Players at Lord's and 100 for England against India at Old Trafford ... No matter who he was with, or where it was, or when, he was always the same man – absolutely fair and as unselfish a captain as England ever had. It is more apparent now that it was at the time that the selectors got rid of him too soon, partly perhaps because he was too independent for their liking. He did things his own way, whatever the establishment may have thought of it.

Towards the end of Vincent's century, the Nawab of Pataudi (junior) hit a hundred in his varsity debut, as his father had done, in 1960 and the next year hit two centuries off the Yorkshire attack which included Fred Trueman, but he was in a car accident before his next varsity game, losing the sight in his right eye. Within a year, he was back, captaining India at the age of 21 and for 40 games. 'He was the first captain to give us a feeling of Indian-ness,' said Bishan Bedi. He was still doing so in the 1970s. The defining moment in the Club's public profile during these years came, however, in athletics. It centred on a Vincent's president, Roger Bannister.

As a student, Roger Bannister did not compete in London 1948 but was the right-hand man to the Oxford-educated organiser of the games, Colonel Evan Hunter. In Helsinki 1952, Bannister came fourth in the 1500 metres. On 6th May 1954, at Iffley Road, he became the first person in history to run a mile in under four minutes. When this former president of the Club and others involved went to Vincent's to celebrate that evening, the fame of the Club was confirmed. The images of a seemingly exhausted and straining Roger Bannister at the finishing line, with much going on inside the track, is an abiding image of greatness in sport, as is the picture of the world's first sub-four-minute miler with his two pacemakers, Chris Chataway and Chris Brasher, shortly afterwards, a byword for fellowship in sport.

Only six years before, when he was an undergraduate and had been elected the president of the Oxford University Athletic Club just before the London Olympics, Roger Bannister had declared that he 'would not rest until plans were started to replace the old ⅓-mile track with a new six-lane 440 yards track conforming to international specifications', because 'the existing track was a disgrace to a University that had produced so many fine athletes'. It was not only the wrong distance but it was undulating – and students ran the wrong way round it. Something had to be done. Roger Bannister saw that and made it happen.

The timekeepers and announcers on 6 May 1954 included the McWhirter twin brothers, Norris and Ross. The overall official in charge of the meeting was Sandy Duncan, also of Vincent's. His obituary in *The Times* begins,

Sandy Duncan was one of the most distinguished and sympathetic sports officials of his generation. For many years he was synonymous with the Olympic movement in Britain, where his common sense in a period of frequent turmoil was valuable. Duncan was this country's chef de mission at 12 winter and summer games, was general secretary of the British Olympic Association (BOA) from 1949 to 1975 and also honorary secretary of the Commonwealth Games Federation, overseeing the celebrations from Vancouver in 1954 to Brisbane in 1982 ... A hamstring injury prevented him from being selected for the Olympics in 1936, so he was attached to the headquarters staff in Berlin, thus beginning his long relationship with the Olympic movement ... His administrative career began in 1947 when he was made secretary of the Universities' Athletic Union. This gave him the initial experience for his appointment, two years later, at the BOA. The following 26 years were difficult ... Despite his BOA post, he still found time to officiate at meetings, including Roger Bannister's first sub-four minute mile in 1954 and the annual Oxford and Cambridge match. He served as secretary of the Achilles Club ... for 39 years ... He was given the rare Olympic Award from the IOC in 1984.

Much has been written about the runners in that Iffley Road mile and the track officials, such as the announcer of the world's first sub-four-minute mile, Norris McWhirter. It is not only the famous Oxbridge alumni running for the AAA that day who have told their stories. The film footage and still photos, as well as many accounts of the race, record that Roger Bannister fell exhausted across the finishing line into the arms of someone. Who was that? It was a friend of his, Nicholas Stacey of St Edmund Hall and Vincent's. Nick Stacey had set a varsity record in 1949 in the 220 yards and competed in the 1952 Helsinki Olympics, including as part of the fifth-placed 4x400 metres relay team. He went on to be an Anglican priest, deputy director of Oxfam and director of social services for Kent County Council. He wrote that as an undergraduate his social life centred around Vincent's and the Gridiron, and when he was revising for Finals, he used to eat in Vincent's with Donald Carr, who was president of Vincent's in the year following Bannister, captaining the Oxford cricket team and later becoming another member to be one of Wisden's cricketers of the year, in 1960, and then a leading administrator of the game in the 1960s and 1970s.

What about the person inside the track who is seen with a clipboard and seeming to cover his head with his hands as Bannister breaks the record, possibly because he cannot bear to watch or, more probably, because he was overcome with emotion? He was Charles Wenden, another Vincent's member, an Oxford Blue half-miler and running friend of Roger Bannister from their early days at Oxford. Although known to his friends as Charles, he wrote as an historian under his actual initials, D J, and was known to some colleagues as David. The confusion arose first at a school sports day where the announcer mistakenly said that Charles Wenden had won, but Charles stuck as a nickname. D J Wenden wrote the chapter on sport in the Oxford University Press's history of the University of Oxford in the last century. He wrote about the history of film, including the book, *The Birth of the Movies*. He had been awarded the Military Cross himself in the Second World War, before he became a student, and wrote much later to put the record straight on All Souls in the run-up to that war, showing that it was not pivotal for the policy of appeasement, as had been suggested. Likewise, he demolished claims that Churchill's famous wartime broadcasts were reconstructions by an actor. Charles Wenden liked to get the record right, as befits a bursar of St Catherine's and of All Souls. Although he corrected the record in relation to appeasement and Churchill, he could also see a value in creativity. He pointed out the inaccuracies in the film *Battleship Potemkin* but nonetheless celebrated the way it gave its own insight into the spirit of the 1905 revolution. Perhaps this can serve as a way of approaching some of the myths and legends of Vincent's, or sporting or social or University life more generally, gently seeking to establish the facts without failing to appreciate the value of symbolism in stories that have occasionally over-dramatised reality.

The reality was in this case worthy of a film. We know that on 6 May 1954, Charles Wenden collected his friend, Roger Bannister, from the station, drove him to Iffley Road and walked him round the track, in a wind that Bannister described as 'almost gale force', before taking him home to lunch with Charles's wife, Eileen, and their daughters, Felicity and Sally. In Bannister's words, 'Absorbed in watching the endless small routine of running a home and family, I could forget some of my apprehensions'. This was not the first time he had benefited from this supportive atmosphere, as the Wendens' house 'had become a second home for me during my research studies in Oxford, and the calm efficiency of Eileen had often helped to still my own restless worries. Never was this factor so important as on this day'.

After his death, St Catherine's celebrated Charles Wenden's commitment to student sport in this way:

> Sport is an important part of life for many students. In order to support our athletes and teams so that they are able to train and compete more effectively, we are looking for further support for the Charles Wenden Fund, which is named in honour of the College's first bursar – a keen sportsman who supported the athletic ambitions of generations of students …

including, it might be added, stints as the honorary treasurer of the national and international organisations for student sport, initially known as BUSF in the UK, subsequently BUSA and now BUCS.

Chris Chataway was one of Roger Bannister's pacemakers, along with Chris Brasher of Cambridge, later an Olympic gold medallist in the steeplechase at Helsinki 1956 and the founder of the London Marathon. Chataway was leading into the final bend of an Olympic 5000 metres final when he fell and got up to finish fifth. Chataway nevertheless won silver at the European Championships 5000 metres and gold in the Empire Games 3 miles. He beat Bannister later in 1954 to the inaugural BBC Sports Personality of the Year award, principally because he had in the autumn beaten the great Vladimir Kuts in a thrilling televised race at the White City. In 1954, the fledgling television programme *Sportsview* piggy-backed the award on a weekly sporting newspaper, *Sporting Record*, which already gave annual awards at a gala dinner. The newspaper's winners that year were Roger Bannister as the *Sporting Record* Sportsman of the Year and Pat Smythe, a show-jumper, as the *Sporting Record* Sportswoman of 1954. The BBC, however, asked the public to vote by sending in postcards, and this led to Bannister coming second and Smythe third, but the surprise winner of the Sportsview poll was Christopher Chataway. The following year he broke the three-mile world record and became the first presenter of the news on ITV. He had worked for Guinness, where he recommended the arrangement with the McWhirters for the famous *Guinness Book of Records* and by the end of the decade he was a Conservative MP. He later he became a government minister, then chairman of the Civil Aviation Authority and has helped various charities. A high-flyer, he was knighted for services to aviation.

Chataway, Brasher, Stacey, Wenden, the McWhirters and Bannister himself had all known what it was like to bounce back from a disappointment in sport. This was never better expressed than by another Vincent's president of the 1950s, Derek Johnson, perhaps the most anti-establishment and truculent of Vincent's presidents. He won silver in the 800 metres and bronze in the 4 x 400 in the Melbourne 1956 Olympics. On the threshold of Rome 1960, he looked back on that 1956 final lap of the 800 metres and wrote profoundly about the experience:

> An Olympic Games is ... a fixed and immutable occasion. It is a sentence as well as an inspiration. We are inspired by the incentive, the challenge and the meaning; we are at the same time sentenced to produce the sum total of our talent, application and character – and luck – on one specified and rapidly approaching day. There is no retreat and no second chance .... I entered the final of the Olympic 800-metres in Melbourne knowing that I had a very fair chance of winning an Olympic gold medal. I failed by one tenth of a second – about a foot in actual distance. For eighty yards of the final straight I led Tom Courtney, the American winner, by the same amount. Tom Courtney was an Olympic champion in the finest sense of the word. He had gathered his deepest resources at a time when many a man would have ceded the race, and had hurled his massive frame past me in the last few strides. I had failed, and failed to achieve the ambition which had meant so much to me. It was a bitter disappointment, and in some ways it still is. But it was a worthwhile disappointment, and were I to be given the same chance again only to face the same outcome I should have no hesitation in seizing it gratefully, for I believe it is important to take whatever talent we have and to use it to the best of our ability.

Other sports and cultures continued to make an impact on the Club. The president of Vincent's in 1954 was R K Pitamber, a golfer from India who has gone on to run India's largest tractor-and-jeep company, Mahindra & Mahindra, and to lead it into a $600 million joint venture with Ford some 40 years after his leadership role in the Club. J C Masterman did not seem to welcome the prospect of Pitamber's election as president and improperly sought to promote another candidate, but the independent streak of the current members prevailed and Pitamber was elected.

Meanwhile, in rugby, the 1950s ended with a spectacular experiment. Pete Dawkins' application of an American Football technique to rugby at the end of the 1950s was foreshadowed in the early 1920s by another American Vincent's member, Alan Chester Valentine. A Rhodes Scholar at Balliol, Valentine won Blues in 1923, 1924 and 1925, as well as a gold medal playing rugby for the USA at the Paris 1924 Olympics. Valentine used the torpedo pass (albeit passing backwards) while the ball was in open play. Just as Bosanquet was accused of being unsporting when developing the googly, the rugby authorities took a dim view of Valentine's technique and Valentine agreed to stop using the throw. Valentine became president of the University of Rochester, New York.

The idea was resurrected, however, in the form of over-arm throwing into line-outs by Oxford in the 1959 varsity match against Cambridge before a large Twickenham crowd of 58,000. David Frost's *The Bowring Story of the Varsity Match* shows that the standard of both teams was awesome, with Cambridge's fly-half, for example, being the Scottish international full-back Ken Scotland, who later played for the British & Irish Lions, while Oxford's fly-half, Richard Sharp, went on to score one of the most celebrated of England tries. Oxford's flankers were Robin (later Sir and now Lord) Butler and the Australian international, Tom Baxter. Butler went on to become the Cabinet secretary and Head of the Civil Service, then Master of University College. Baxter had played on the wing for Australia against New Zealand in 1958 and for Oxford against Cambridge in the 1958 Varsity match but he played wing-forward in 1959. It was a player new to rugby, however, who inspired and executed a new tactic. Oxford practised it in secret and unleashed it in their game of the season. Until then, wingers had thrown in the ball and mostly did it two-handed and under-arm. Pete Dawkins threw the ball one-handed and over-arm. He threw it way over the forwards to be caught in mid-field by his centre and captain, Vincent's Malcolm Phillips, who had already played for England and who was to become president of the Club and of the RFU. This was a time when the opposing three-quarters did not have to be 20 metres apart at a line-out so there was little space, but the element of surprise worked, Phillips twice taking the ball cleanly from a perfect throw of 40 yards to make ground. There was a concern that referees would err on the side of caution and judge long throws as 'not straight' but the tactic was accepted by the Twickenham referee. Oxford won the game 9-3, all penalties. It was no mean feat to break into this team at all. While the international Baxter had been on one wing in 1958, the other winger from 1956 to 1958 was Vincent's J R C Young, who was the AAA sprint champion and England international rugby player who in 1959 played well for the British & Irish Lions on their tour of New Zealand and Australia. Baxter, the continuing Blue winger and an international, moved into the pack to accommodate the newcomer.

Pete Dawkins is the only Rhodes Scholar in history to have won the Heisman Trophy for the most outstanding college player in American Football. He played other sports at West Point, the elite US army officer college, and Oxford won a half-Blue in one of them, ice hockey. When he arrived at Brasenose College, he was encouraged to play rugby and quickly went on to the Greyhounds, the University 2nd XV, and then the University's first team, scoring two tries on his debut and playing well in the high-profile game against Major Stanley's XV, which led to his selection in his very first term of rugby to play against Cambridge. He was not selected just for this tactic but went on to play in two further Varsity matches. After leaving Oxford, Pete Dawkins became a Vietnam war hero, winning medals and retiring as a US brigadier general, failing in a bid to become a Senator but succeeding at the highest levels in yet another sphere, this time in banking. In 2009, he summed up his education thus: 'At West Point, it's all about solving problems and you get very good at being able to solve more and more complex problems. Oxford is the opposite. Oxford is all about identifying what are the key questions. When you put both of them together, it really suited me well.'

This era ends with Richard Sharp captaining England, introducing the team to the Prime Minister, Harold Macmillan, and going on to score a spectacular try at Twickenham as England won what would now be called the grand slam in 1963. Presidents and the extraordinary 'ordinary' members of the Club have often been mentioned in this account, but just as the 1950s began with a brilliant double international as club secretary in Clive van Ryneveld, so the century ended with the heroics of another secretary in Richard Sharp. He has explained his life as a student:

> I worked hard in the mornings and most evenings. The afternoons were devoted to
> sport. I did not go to parties other than the occasional College club dinner, nor did
> I drink alcohol. I needed to work in the evenings and I did not have enough money
> or time to socialise much. Playing rugby for England took up considerable time in

the Hilary terms. Fortunately there were only four England matches in those days and the demands on the players were considerably less than they are today in the professional era. One day I would be playing for England at Twickenham, or in Paris, and three days later I would be playing for Balliol at Cuppers in the parks! When there were no matches, I went training every afternoon. One of the great advantages of Balliol in the early 1960s was that it was possible to return from playing for England at Twickenham and to be asked by someone in the JCR where I had been for the weekend! This in no way dismayed me ... Happily, I was able to play cricket for Balliol in the summer on a regular basis, except in the year of my final examinations, when I played no cricket at all. Playing cricket for the College gave me as much pleasure as my rugby. I have still got the fixture list for the 1961 season, when I was Captain ... I am rather shocked to see that we had 22 matches in that Trinity Term, which seems rather a lot of cricket in an eight-week term. Ten of those matches started at 11.30am.

He has said of the photograph of him greeting the then Prime Minister Harold Macmillan, 'I think it might have been the only game of rugby he ever attended'. The papers were full of praise for the 'gliding majesty of the blond-haired lead character' (Sharp, not Macmillan), 'Three sidesteps, natural spatial awareness, startling pace', and he scored a majestic try by finding the gaps in the Scottish defence: 'I wouldn't have wanted to play professional rugby because I had other interests but I'd have enjoyed being a player now. They're all so much better, fitter and stronger. I admire them all, although many seem to run into people deliberately. When I was young we were always looking for gaps rather than contact.'

The questions arise, after such an eventful 50 years, whether Vincent's could remain in contact with its alumni and whether there were any gaps in its history of pioneers and heroes through which the next generation could glide? The answer is hinted at in one of the most endearing accounts of how Vincent's would seem to any young student, given the weight of its history. For at the beginning of the post-war glories of Vincent's, it had seemed intimidating even to one of sport's greatest-ever characters, Sir Roger Bannister, who recalled his first memories of the Club thus:

I had always been puzzled by the mysterious institution called 'Vincent's' – to which the more pleasant and sociable athletes would disappear when overwhelmed by success or failure ... The members were mainly sportsmen – sport tends to produce a more sociable person than pure scholarship. There were few full Blues who were not members, so my fellow athletes were keen to have me elected. I was absurdly young for such an honour and felt supremely 'unclubbable' ... One day I was taken there to dine by a committee member, R T S Macpherson ... I quaked at finding myself in company with such Oxford heroes – in my nervousness I upset my tankard and hardly ate anything. I heard later that I had been elected a member. For nearly a year I hardly decided to go inside the club ... I had such veneration for the club's tradition that I was quite unable to relax in it. Three years later when I was president of the club and lived in a room there, I found Vincent's one of Oxford's most enjoyable institutions.

CHAPTER 4

1963–2013: The High-Flyers

The year 1963 was an *annus mirabilis*, according to Philip Larkin: '… life was never better than in nineteen sixty-three … between the end of the Chatterley ban and the Beatles' first LP'. But how could life, or the next 50 years, be better or even as good for Vincent's after the pioneering of 1863–1913 and then the heroics of 1913–63? Various factors are assumed by doom-mongers to have contributed to a downturn in the fortunes of Oxford sport and Vincent's. The standard of sport in the University has allegedly declined, with the coming of professionalism in, for instance, rugby union and with the funding available for Olympic prospects, so that the old amateur days of combining sport and study have supposedly gone. With the advent of £9,000 annual fees at undergraduate level and the difficulties of the global economy since 2008, students are said to focus much more on their degree results and career options. We would never see such heady days, on this reckoning, as when the previous chapter concluded with, as we have seen, the Prime Minister, Harold Macmillan, being introduced to the England rugby union team by their captain, Richard Sharp, so recently a Vincent's committee member, on 16 March 1963 and then Sharp scoring one of the greatest tries ever seen at Twickenham or anywhere else to win the match.

Now that was indeed sublime, but was it really as good as it could possibly get for Vincent's? This chapter takes politicians from the beginning, middle and end of these 50 years to show how Vincent's alumni continue to have an impact in politics and to draw on their student experiences. Then examples will be given from the ranks of other politicians, diplomats, civil servants and business leaders to illustrate other high-flying careers. To get a sense of the broad sweep of Oxford sport over these 50 years, rugby will be briefly contrasted with rowing, and a jockey and an angler will be given extended consideration on either side of a brief indication of how high recent members might fly in the next 50 years. This means going forwards and backwards through the half-century, but that is to counter the assumptions that sports and characters are in decline at Oxford. Rather, there are many more sporting outlets and even more diverse characters. In many ways, it has been business as usual for Vincent's, the primary differences being simply that readers are closer to the events of the last period while the recent graduates have not yet had the time since their student days to make their mark in the wider world.

In the mid-60s, if there was a defining description of the physical Club, rather than of the great individual members and their collective metaphysical influence, it could be in a brilliant book about Oxford by an alumnus of the University, a writer of distinction who was fit enough as a young journalist to have accompanied the Everest expedition in 1954, and ingenious enough to have brought news of its success to the world on the very eve of the coronation of Queen Elizabeth. Writing at the beginning of Vincent's latest 50 years, in 1965, James Morris (now Jan Morris CBE) generously observed that 'you may generally find an Olympic runner or two in the bar at Vincent's'. He then set the Club in the context of carrying forward the spirit of Matthew Arnold and the Oxford ethos of the 19th century:

> The ideal of the Renaissance man was still alive in those days, and in Oxford it was interpreted as the cult of the jolly good all-rounder. You may still meet him now and then, and especially in the famous old club called Vincent's, in upstairs premises off the High. This is pre-eminently a sporting club, but its members were to be elected, so the original statutes said in 1863, for their 'all-round qualities – social, physical and intellectual qualities being duly considered' ... at Vincent's whose walls are lined with photographs of eminent members, and whose undergraduate membership is limited to 150 at a time, you may still feel the allure of that old philosophy ... It is mellow and unexpectedly subtle. It is named after the printer whose shop happened to be on the floor below the original premises. Its committee invented the kind of tie that has the pattern of crests all over it .... In an England of shifting convictions, Vincent's feels supremely sure of itself ...

Sure enough, in politics, for instance, Vincent's members in 1963 to 2013 have more than matched earlier vintages, and not only in England. Beginning with the Westminster government, however, the new era was off to a spectacular start in the autumn of 1963 when the Prime Ministership passed from one Vincent's member (albeit an honorary one) to another, from the University of Oxford's Chancellor to a former Vincent's president, from Harold Macmillan to Sir Alec Douglas-Home. ITN News wanted to know what kind of person the new Prime Minister was. So they went to interview one of his former tutors at Christ Church, now the Provost of Worcester, and a fellow Vincent's member, Sir John Masterman:

Q: What was his reputation as a student at Christ Church?

A: Well I think everybody liked him enormously. He was liked and he was respected by everyone. And not only by people of one kind only. I remember very well one undergraduate, whom I knew well and who held rather advanced or radical views, saying to me once 'Oh you know Alex Douglas, as Lord Home then was, Alex Douglas is the only valid reason that I have for not wishing for the abolition of the Lords'. I can think of other reasons for that, but it's not a bad one. I think he was universally liked and universally respected too. Of course he had many activities outside Christ Church as well. He was President of Vincent's Club, which is about the highest social position you can find in the University amongst undergraduates and he was a very good cricketer. He played several times for the University, he might easily have got a Blue, he didn't, but then that happens in these cases.

In these five minutes or so on the evening ITN News of 18 September 1963, Sir John and Sir Alec brought Vincent's once again to centre stage. Sir John explained that he shared responsibility for Sir Alec with another Christ Church don, Sir Keith Feiling, who was also a Vincent's member. When Feiling had written about Christ Church men of distinction over the centuries, the one he knew was Lord Rosebery – the previous Prime Minister to have been a member of Vincent's, the one who left the University as horse-racing was more important to him. When judging the performance of any Vincent's president or member in this most recent half-century, it is worth bearing in mind that Sir Alec Douglas-Home took 40 years from being president to fly to the top of politics. Of course, he had not been idle in between times. Indeed, he had taken one of the most famous, or infamous, return flights in political history. When Alec Douglas-Home was Neville Chamberlain's Parliamentary Private secretary, he had to accompany the Prime Minister to the notorious meeting with Adolf Hitler in Munich in 1938. He did not have time to pack but borrowed a shirt from his brother's flat-mate, another Vincent's member, Brian Johnston, who became a famously jovial and accomplished cricket commentator and media personality.

It is regularly recounted that Alec Douglas-Home was the only Prime Minister of the United Kingdom to have played first-class cricket. This is true and it is also the case that he played for the University while at Oxford but, as he was the first to point out, he was dropped after the last game before the varsity match. As he explains in his autobiography, *The Way the Wind Blows*, this was because he was hit for 'three consecutive and towering sixes' by Percy Perrin of Essex. So he was not awarded a Blue. His ten first-class cricket games came for six sides, as Wisden records:

> Middlesex, Oxford University, H D G Leveson Gower's XI, MCC (with whom he toured South America under Pelham Warner), Free Foresters and Harlequins. His two games for Middlesex were in 1924 and 1925, both against Oxford University while he was actually an Oxford undergraduate; he did not represent the university until the following year.

He seems to have enjoyed his cricket both as a player and when he became president of MCC in 1966. In his autobiography, he says of J C Masterman: 'J C was an extremely good games-player', but, 'Perhaps J C was too tolerant of my passion for cricket – not that I regret for one moment the part which games and sport have played in my life. I am unrepentant in my belief that "team games" for the young are good for body, mind and soul'.

Given the assumption nowadays that politicians can be blown about in the wind, it is worth pointing out that the title of Lord Home's autobiography has a different meaning altogether, more related to 'sport' as understood by John Buchan and Sir Edward Grey. While one journalist was interviewing Sir John Masterman, another was asking the Home family's head gamekeeper about the new Prime Minister. He said that the Home boys 'always seem to know which way the wind blows', which is about as high-flying an expression of praise as he could give, because, as Lord Home explained: '… my father was a countryman, and a naturalist, and on the right interpretation of wind or weather depended the action of the day. So every morning, as soon as we could walk, our first conscious act was to look and see which way the wind blew. It mattered a lot.' It is this sense, translated from field sports to spotting what is going to happen next in a team game or in politics or business, that is one of the most intangible but vital abilities in many spheres of life. It cannot be learned quickly but matures as an understanding through experience and mentoring. In much the same way, those selectors in the game of life, for example in politics or finance or business, who place some value on the sporting accomplishments of Vincent's members and their student involvement in leadership, are not merely granting favours based on a club tie. They can themselves be demonstrating a shrewd understanding of the way the wind blows, like the Home boys, Alec who became Prime Minister and Charles, whose flatmate Brian Johnston lent Alec the shirt.

If political leadership is the test, any assumption that Vincent's influence has been on the wane in the last 50 years is mistaken. In an era of high-flyers and jet-setters, Australia provides a counter-example in the middle of this latest half-century, with another Vincent's man becoming Prime Minister in the federal election of September 2013, the Club's 150th anniversary year. Labour's Bob Hawke was elected Prime Minister of Australia four times, in 1983, 1984, 1987 and 1990. On the other side of Australia's political spectrum, the Prime Minister of Australia elected in 2013 is the leader of the Liberal party, another Vincent's man, Tony Abbott. Their Oxford sporting and drinking days have become a legendary part of their stories, which the media in Australia re-tell frequently. Bob Hawke, in particular, is credited with a world record for drinking beer, as recorded in the Guinness Book of World Records, compiled by Vincent's men from the same era, Norris and Ross McWhirter. In Bob Hawke's own memoirs, he does not mention Vincent's in 600 pages, although he does talk about University College, his thesis, learning to fly at the Oxford University Air Squadron and playing cricket (or often being twelfth man for the University) in the 1950s.

In the biography of him by Blanche d'Alpuget, however, the Club does appear. When Hawke was prosecuted for dangerous driving, after an Air Squadron dinner, a story Hawke relates himself, d'Alpuget adds a Vincent's detail or two: 'already he was something of a hero, a Wild Colonial Boy, to sections of the student community, particularly those in the sporting club, Vincent's.' The police shocked Hawke, apparently, by lying about an obscene gesture he was said to have made through his car window. He was convicted. He appealed and by the time that was to be heard in March 1955 he had been convicted and fined £5 for attempting to steal a street lamp in another escapade. He wanted to win the appeal without opening up the possibility of the police being able to inform the court and the media of this other incident. His barrister, Oliver Popplewell, was a member of Hawk's, the nearest equivalent to Vincent's at Cambridge, who asked the policemen to tell the judge whether the car window, out of which Hawke was alleged to have made an obscene gesture to them, was fully down or not. One said it was, one said it was three-quarters down. The judge could see that at least one of the policemen was unreliable and the truth, as Hawke had told Popplewell, was that the window could not be opened up or down in the manner they were claiming. The court was packed with supporters. All it needed now was for Hawke's friend, fellow cricketer and Vincent's member, Jimmy Allan, to turn up as a witness, but d'Alpuget tells us he was late. The court had to adjourn. Allan rushed in without a tie and in some versions is given a Hawk's one. According to d'Alpuget, Allan was defiant when chided by the judge for being late. Allan said he had been playing rugby. The judge was unimpressed until he realised that Jimmy Allan was playing a Cuppers final for Worcester, his and the judge's old college. Hawke was soon vindicated and there were celebrations. Popplewell later became a judge and conducted the inquiry into the tragedy of the Bradford Football Club fire. On retirement, he decided to return to study, for fun, this time to Oxford. Although Popplewell would have had reciprocal rights anyway as a Hawk's member, Vincent's elected him as an honorary member, a rare example of such dual citizenship.

Almost any minor incident of such a nature involving one Vincent's man could show further connections which create a picture of sport and wider life at the time and in subsequent decades. Vincent's members who might not be household names in one era can feature in the stories of those who become famous in another. For example, and this is not mentioned by the Australian writers, the witness, Jimmy Allan, had played in May 1953 in only his second match for Oxford against the Australians, who included Keith Miller and Richie Benaud. Allan was at number eleven and did not score in what was his second game for the University. He had been 12 not out in his debut against Yorkshire earlier that month, also batting at eleven. As that batting position suggests, of course, he was in the side for his bowling. Colin Cowdrey takes up the story:

> We had an exciting game with the Australians, considering the relative strength of the two sides and considering that we were bowled out for 70 on a drying wicket

on the first day. The Australians in their turn were 62 for 4 largely through a remarkable first over by Jimmy Allan. He had played in the previous match against Yorkshire and had bowled seven overs, all maidens, for one wicket. He began with another maiden against the Australians and in it took two wickets. At that moment he had taken the wickets of Vic Wilson – the week before – Keith Miller and Ian Craig and had yet to concede a run in first-class cricket.

Allan played under Cowdrey's captaincy for Oxford against Yorkshire in the Parks in the following season, in May 1954, when the weather was so bad that there was no play on the scheduled first day, 5 May. On the next day, Hutton was out for only 21, but Allan's figures were 0 for 77 when Yorkshire declared on 293 for 4. Their bowling attack of Trueman, Yardley, Wardle, Close and Illingworth reduced Oxford to 35 for 9 before Allan, now batting at number nine, was involved in a last wicket stand that took the university to 58 all out. It would be good to think that Trueman, who took 5 for 8 off 10 overs, and the rest of the Yorkshire team joined Allan, Cowdrey and the Oxford players at Vincent's for a drink alongside Roger Bannister, Chris Chataway and others from Iffley Road who had made history that evening in the first mile run in under four minutes. Cowdrey, at least, has written about being there in Vincent's on the evening of 6 May. Encouraged by Bannister's success, no doubt, Oxford saved the game the next day, scoring 239.

Allan's chance to move up the order came the next month when he was night-watchman in a game against Hampshire, so that neither J P 'Pom-Pom' Fellows-Smith nor the captain Colin Cowdrey would have to bat that evening. Allan survived and went on to score a century the next day in partnership with Charles (now Lord) Williams, also of Vincent's, who achieved his highest first-class score of 139 not out. Williams captained Oxford the next year, in succession to Cowdrey. After a career in the oil industry and banking, he became chair of the Prices Commission in the last years of the Labour government of Jim Callaghan, before becoming a Labour peer in 1985 and serving in such roles as deputy leader of Labour in the Lords and as Labour's spokesman on trade. Some newspapers in 2013 have noticed that Lord Williams' stepson, Justin Welby, seems at first to have followed his stepfather's career path in oil and finance, although instead of going into party politics he has joined the House of Lords on the episcopal benches, becoming the Bishop of Durham and now in 2013 the Archbishop of Canterbury.

Meanwhile, Allan was promoted to open with M J K Smith and scored 150 against Sussex, including a partnership of 212 with Colin Cowdrey, who scored 140. Allan opened in the varsity match with M J K Smith, scoring 86 while Mike Smith went on to a double century. Allan became disillusioned with cricket for Kent, having been recommended to the county by Cowdrey, and returned to a business career in his native Scotland, occasionally playing cricket for Scotland. In this latest half a century of Vincent's, Jimmy Allan was still good enough at the end of the 1966 season to have played for the International Cavaliers, cricket's nearest equivalent to rugby's Barbarians, against a West Indies XI that included Gary Sobers. Jimmy Allan was back down the order but the people ahead of him were Saeed Ahmed, Mervyn Kitchen, Ted Dexter, Graeme Pollock, Denis Compton, Trevor Bailey and two wicket-keeper-batsmen, Jim Parks and Godfrey Evans. Allan was 14 not out and had the best bowling analysis with 4 for 34 as the Cavaliers won this pioneering example of limited-over cricket.

For our purposes, the more important point is that a character witness for Bob Hawke was a fellow Vincent's member and a cricketing Blue who stopped off on his way to the court case to play in the rugby Cuppers final for his college. If he did not fly as high as some in later life, he certainly rose through the Oxford batting order to perform at a high standard in the most illustrious company. Meanwhile, Worcester lost that game and have not yet won rugby Cuppers, despite having a ground inside their college and having the most distinguished of rugby players as an alumnus, David Kirk of New Zealand, the first captain to win the World Cup and another member of Vincent's.

By the time Bob Hawke had won his second federal election, in the mid-1980s another Australian Rhodes Scholar was appearing for Oxford in sport. In 1984, Oxford boxing was casting around not so much for a high-flyer or flyweight or political heavyweight, but just anyone brave enough to complete the team to face Cambridge. As a rugby player in the front row for the University of Sydney, a Rhodes Scholar called Tony Abbott had thought it prudent to take some boxing lessons. Now he was given a skipping rope and encouraged to get fit.

At the end of 2012, as leader of the opposition Liberal Party, Australia's equivalent to the Conservatives, Abbott returned to Queen's College for a lecture which gave the media back in Australia the opportunity to run headlines such as 'Not the greatest, but a fighter'. One newspaper, reporting the 2012 speech, tells the story of Oxford boxing in the 1980s:

Oxford saw another Abbott: the colonial gorilla in the boxing ring. Abbott became famous at university for his performance in the Oxford-Cambridge boxing match when, with the varsity battle locked 4-4 and the heavyweight bout the decider, he climbed into the ring for his first fight. He had been sick with nerves in the hours beforehand, fearing what sort of trouble lay ahead. When the referee issued the instruction 'Box!' Abbott operated on pure instinct. He applied the principle he has many times since: 'Kill or be killed.' He flayed his taller opponent with a flurry of blows in what participants at the event recall as hardly elegant but effective. After 45 seconds of the first round in a three-round contest, he landed a serious blow; his opponent went down, and was knocked out. A win for the colonial gorilla at his first outing.

This is not quite the same as the way in which the Australian rower, sculler, Olympian, war hero and musician, F S Kelly, was typecast as rather muscular in his piano-playing by a music critic. Just as Hawke encouraged stories about his Oxford days, so Abbott knows what he is doing in cultivating the boxing imagery, feeding the lines to the media. He is not only a high-flyer but has made play of flying low:

> Like about a million other Australian, including Prime Minister Gillard, who also came to Australia as a child, I was born in Britain ... So when the plane bringing me back to Britain flew low up the Thames Valley and I saw for the first time as an adult Westminster Abbey, the Houses of Parliament, St Paul's Cathedral and the Tower of London, I had a sense of belonging, not because I was born here but because our culture was ... when I was the successful heavyweight in the annual varsity match and knocked out my opponent after 45 seconds of round one, a[n] ... Englishman commented: what could you expect when we import gorillas from the colonies?

At the end of 2009, when Abbott became leader, another Australian newspaper had given his complete boxing history:

> In his first bout, against Cambridge, he knocked his opponent out cold in 45 seconds. His second, against a cadet officer from Sandhurst Royal Military College,

was also over in the first round. His third bout, against a marine who had fought in the Falklands War and 'a much bigger man', was won by Abbott on a TKO [technical knock-out] when his opponent took his fifth standing count in the second round. In the fourth and final fight of his career, he triumphed for the second time over a Cambridge man – the bout again being stopped in the first round.

Tony Abbott became Prime Minister of Australia in September 2013. This gives a fitting declaration of the continuing influence of Vincent's members in public life. The Club's association with Macmillan, as an honorary member, and Douglas-Home, as a former president, at the time of its centenary has played a great part in the legendary status of Vincent's. There was a danger, however, that this half-century would be seen as having nowhere to go but down from a high-water mark of political achievement. Instead, Hawke and now Abbott have shown that if the trajectory is down it is only in the sense of Down Under. A better way of looking at the development over 150 years is that if the founder was at times considered to be a little parochial, having only ever ventured abroad once, to a rowing regatta in Paris, the Club now is confirmed as having a global reach.

Nor is it simply the party leaders and Prime Ministers – Alec Douglas-Home in 1963, Bob Hawke in the 1980s through to 1991 and now Tony Abbott in 2013 – who have been Vincent's only politicians in the Club's latest half-century. At the start of this period, for example, Bill Bradley won basketball gold at Tokyo 1964 Olympics for the USA, then studied at Oxford as a Rhodes Scholar, winning his Blue, became a member of Vincent's, played professional basketball for the New York Knicks from 1967 to 1977, twice winning the NBA Finals, then served as Senator from 1979 to 1997 and ran for the Democrat nomination to be president in 2000, losing to Al Gore. He has also turned his hand to many non-executive roles in business and to many campaigns for the disadvantaged in America.

In the UK, there are Vincent's alumni who have been MPs for a considerable time and some who have featured briefly in the Commons. Bill Cash, the Eurosceptic Conservative MP, has been in Parliament since 1984 and Sir Edward Garnier, recently the Solicitor-General, since 1992. Sometimes a more fleeting experience can betoken a high-flying career in more than politics; sometimes it is because a talented individual has flown too close to the sun. Jeffrey Archer was president of the Oxford University Athletics Club and a committee member of

Vincent's at the start of this period, then an MP for five years from 1969, a Tory peer in 1992 and deputy chairman of the Conservative party in 1995. He was the Conservative candidate for London mayor when news broke in 1999 of his perjury and perverting the course of justice in an earlier libel case against the *Daily Star* commenting on a *News of the World* story. He was convicted in 2001, but on release from prison has resumed his career as a novelist and is now said to have sold over a quarter of a billion copies of his books. He is also a considerable philanthropist, including as a benefactor to Oxford sporting causes. Lord Archer is best known within Vincent's for his role in bringing the Beatles to the Club in 1964, when he had persuaded them to perform in a charity event for Oxfam. The picture of that occasion, of the Beatles at the bar of the Club, had pride of place in Vincent's bar.

Another meteoric high-flyer among Vincent's politicians is Colin Moynihan, who pre-dated Tony Abbott in rising from the ranks of Vincent's boxers. In 1977, Colin Moynihan was a double Blue, as cox in the boat race and as a bantamweight boxer, as well as a Vincent's member and president of the Oxford Union. He worked in business for Tate & Lyle, served as an MP from 1983 to 1992, then in the House of Lords, having succeeded by a distant and contested route to an hereditary peerage. He won silver as a cox in the Moscow 1980 Olympics, defying Margaret Thatcher's call for a boycott, but still became her minister for sport later in the 1980s. In 2005 Lord Moynihan was elected Chairman of the British Olympic Association and was re-elected, so that he covered the period from the year of London being awarded the Games right through to the successes of London 2012 itself.

Hawke was a Labour politician, Bradley a Democrat, but these best-known British examples of Vincent's politicians listed above are Conservatives. There is, however, a Liberal Democrat waiting in the wings, and the more recent Vincent's members include some who would be more comfortable in the Labour party. Reg Clark, Vincent's president in 1980, was treasurer of the Liberal Democrats from 2000 to 2005. Clark is a leading example of Vincent's high-flyers who have pioneered the huge expansion in the burgeoning international business of sport, in his case as the chief executive of Rhino, makers and sellers of sporting equipment, from kit to artificial pitches to their famous scrummage machines and rugby balls. In 2013, they provided the kit for the Barbarians and the match balls for the

British & Irish Lions' match against the Barbarians in Hong Kong, as well as being the commercial match-ball providers for the 2013 rugby league World Cup to be played in the UK. Rhino are generous in their support of students and of pioneers in sport, donating the kit for the annual varsity rugby league match and now for Oxford's new semi-professional rugby league team, playing at Iffley Road.

Reg Clark has done much with Vincent's to keep the memory of Ambassador Katsuhiko Oku alive and to foster good Anglo-Japanese sporting relations. Ambassador Oku was the first Japanese player to gain a rugby union Blue at Oxford. He would have continued his championing of Japan's wish to host a rugby union world cup, but he was killed while serving in Iraq in 2003 in the attempt to reconstruct that country. An annual rugby tournament, including an all-star team from Vincent's, is a pioneering example of the way in which sport is developing. The influence of an inspirational character is kept alive through his friends banding together, capturing the essence of how he made a difference, and then finding a way to promote that spirit. In 2009, it was decided that Japan would indeed host the rugby World Cup in 2019. Oxford rugby has a fine record in sending touring teams to Japan and hosting teams from Japan. One of the heroes of Oxford sport in the early 1950s, Brian Boobyer, one of Vincent's double Blues in cricket and rugby, gave up his England rugby and stayed in Japan at the end of the University's first tour there in 1952, committing his life to the Moral Re-Armament movement, initially in Japan and other parts of Asia. In 1976, Japan played Oxford at Iffley Road. Vincent's will undoubtedly be represented by Reg Clark and many others when Ambassador Oku's dream comes true in 2019.

More formal diplomacy, including in Anglo-Japanese relations, has been well served by Vincent's members in these past 50 years. For example, the chairman of the Vincent's 150th anniversary appeal, Melville Guest, who represented Oxford in cricket, rackets and rugby union and was president of Vincent's in 1966, joined the Foreign Office in the same year, serving in Tokyo, Paris (and in a senior role in industry there) before returning to Tokyo in 1986. Back in London he became founder chief executive of Asia House London and was awarded the OBE in 2007 for services to the UK's relations with Asia. His doubles partner in the varsity rackets team, Sir Jeremy Greenstock, has explained that Melville Guest's example tempted him to join the Foreign Office a year later to learn Japanese, but in the event he preferred to learn Arabic, as that could be done abroad, in the Lebanon, which was more appealing than the Japanese course, which had just been repatriated to an English university setting. Sir Jeremy was knighted in 1998, having served in a variety of roles in the Middle East, in Washington, London and Bosnia. He became the UK's Permanent Representative to the UN from 1998 up to and including the challenging time of the Iraq War, and then was Special Representative in Baghdad in 2003 and 2004. At the UN he had succeeded (Sir) John Weston, another member, who had an equally distinguished career, having also been UK Permanent Representative to NATO. The current chairman of the Vincent's Appeal Trust Company (the Trustee of the Club) is Sir Ivor Roberts, president of Trinity, who followed suit in studying Arabic in the Lebanon at the end of the 1960s, then took postings all around the world before becoming Ambassador first of all in what was then the Federal Republic of Yugoslavia in the mid-1990s, then in Ireland at the end of the century, and subsequently in Italy in this century. Examples could be multiplied, but perhaps best known of all was Sir Antony Acland, Ambassador in Washington, Head of the Diplomatic Service and later Knight of the Order of the Garter.

At home, leading public servants have included Lords Moore and Butler. Philip Moore scored 197 not out for Cheltenham College against Malvern in 1939, deferred going up to Brasenose and flew as a navigator for Bomber Command, until being hit over France in 1942. As high-flyers go, this is the most spectacular survival story, as re-told in one of his obituaries:

> As he was blown out of the wrecked fuselage, a parachute pack miraculously landed in his lap. He grabbed it and descended safely, the only member of the crew to survive. His luck held at first. He was sheltered by the local French resistance, but then was betrayed to the Germans and spent the next three years as a prisoner of war in Stalag Luft III, famous for its 'wooden horse' escape plan – in which he helped – whereby a vaulting horse was kept in constant use by the British PoWs to mask the excavation of a tunnel under the barbed wire.

Lord Moore won Blues in hockey and rugby after the war and played for England at the latter in 1951. He joined the civil service and worked in the UK and abroad until drawn into Buckingham Palace in 1966, becoming The Queen's personal private secretary in 1977 and serving until he retired in 1986, when he took the suitably Oxonian title of Lord Moore of Wolvercote.

Robin Butler was president of Vincent's in 1961 and a member of famous Oxford rugby teams, members of which also included Richard Sharp and Pete Dawkins. After a First in Greats, he joined the Treasury, and by the 1970s was private secretary to successive Prime Ministers: Ted Heath, Harold Wilson and Margaret Thatcher. Only a dozen years after being Vincent's president, Robin Butler was there at Sunningdale when the first Anglo-Irish Agreement was signed in 1973 by Ted Heath and Liam Cosgrave, and is in the photograph standing behind the two premiers. Another dozen years later, as Margaret Thatcher's principal private secretary, he was famously working with her on government business before she was to turn her attention to writing her speech for the Conservative party conference on the night when their hotel was bombed by the IRA in 1984. As Cabinet secretary later in her administration, and in the governments of John Major and Tony Blair, he was involved in the Northern Irish peace process right through to the Good Friday Agreement in 1998 and beyond. More than a quarter of a century at the highest levels of government justifies the term high-flyer, often applied more loosely to those entering the Treasury or the wider civil service in 'fast stream' or 'fast track' programmes. He was knighted in 1988 and ennobled in 1998, having been the highest of high-flyers in the civil service, working with successive Prime Ministers, ultimately as Cabinet secretary. He became Master of University College and is the Life president of Vincent's.

Although courage could not be shown in quite the same way and on the same scale as during the two world wars, Vincent's members continued to risk their lives. Before Robin Butler survived the Brighton bomb in the 1980s, three Vincent's members were killed by Irish republicans in the 1970s, all of them having chosen to pursue their interests in Northern Ireland despite knowing that they were targets of the terrorists. Ross McWhirter was killed in 1975, Captain Bob Nairac in 1977 and Rt Hon Airey Neave MP in 1979. Ross McWhirter had become a campaigner for freedom, taking up unfashionable causes and putting, as Irish republicans saw it, a bounty on their heads. Bob Nairac is remembered at Oxford for resuscitating the boxing club, before the times of Colin Moynihan and Tony Abbott, winning Blues in each of his four years, and for his commitment to falconry. The boxing club's own history recounts that it was founded in 1881 but

On 22 January 1969, the OUABC committee was forced to disband the club within a few weeks of the Varsity Boxing Match because of declining student interest in boxing and the club's poor financial position. However, one of the boxers, the charismatic Robert Nairac, refused to allow OUABC to die. Along with the help of Julian Malins, he formed a team from thin air by force of personality, knocking on the doors of students and asking them to box. They narrowly lost to Cambridge that year, but the club was saved.

Explanations of Bob Nairac's undercover work and his death have not convinced all concerned that the full story has yet emerged but the flavour is given by the citation when he was awarded the George Cross posthumously:

On the night of 14/15 May 1977 Captain Nairac was abducted from a village in South Armagh by at least seven men. Despite his fierce resistance he was overpowered and taken across the border into the nearby Republic of Ireland where he was subjected to a succession of exceptionally savage assaults in an attempt to extract information which would have put other lives and future operations at serious risk. These efforts to break Captain Nairac's will failed entirely. Weakened as he was in strength – though not in spirit – by the brutality, he yet made repeated and spirited attempts to escape, but on each occasion was eventually overpowered by the weight of the numbers against him. After several hours in the hands of his captors Captain Nairac was callously murdered by a gunman of the Provisional Irish Republican Army who had been summoned to the scene. His assassin subsequently said 'He never told us anything'. Captain Nairac's exceptional courage and acts of the greatest heroism in circumstances of extreme peril showed devotion to duty and personal courage second to none.

Neave had received the Military Cross in the second world war and was well known as having escaped Colditz, before returning to the war effort and ultimately undertaking a series of major roles in the war trials at Nuremberg, where 'Khaki' Roberts of Vincent's was a leading prosecutor and Lord Justice Lawrence, later the first Lord Oaksey, also of Vincent's, was the presiding judge. Paul Routledge in his biography of Neave makes much of an obscure Merton dining club to which Neave belonged, but misses the Vincent's connections. Given J C Masterman's long influence in the Club and his role as the mastermind behind the double cross system in the Second World War, it would be no surprise if one of the reasons for Vincent's paucity of records is that the Club may have been a fertile recruiting-ground for spymasters. Airey Neave had managed Margaret Thatcher's campaign when she became leader of the Conservative party. He was shadow spokesman on Northern Ireland and on the cusp of the 1979 general election when his car was blown up within the precincts of the House of Commons. Giving the first Airey Neave Memorial Lecture in 1980, Margaret Thatcher described him as

> irreplaceable ... His long and varied public service began with one of the most famous feats of the Second World War: his escape from Colditz. He learned much from that extraordinary experience. The prisons of Nazi Germany taught him all that he needed to know about the character of totalitarian rule. Afterwards, Airey did not have to speculate how a brutal police state behaves when freedom falters: he had himself suffered at the hands of the Gestapo. Nor did he have to read Dostoevsky to know what it means to be told (falsely) that he was about to be court-martialled and shot: it had happened to him ... Airey did not need to study history to know the truth about intolerance, for he had seen Jews being, literally, kicked off the pavement into the street in Munich by SS men. He had seen the Nazi movement at its zenith before the Second World War, with its mass marches and compelling fervour. He also saw that movement in its death-throes when, by what he himself described as a strange reversal of fortunes, he, the successful escaped prisoner-of-war, personally served the allied indictment on the major war criminals in their cells at Nuremburg ... During the war itself, Airey Neave's escape gave him many precious intimations of truth. There is a fine passage in his book where he describes how he felt an 'exquisite unburdening of the soul' when he knew that he was, miraculously, outside the prison gates, and free. Airey went on to tell his readers that escape 'is not a technique but a philosophy'.
>
> The real escaper from a prisoner-of-war camp, he said, 'is not just a man equipped with compass, maps and so on. He has an inner self-confidence, a serenity of the spirit, which will make him a pilgrim'.

That would be a good epitaph for many a Vincent's pioneer, hero and high-flyer.

The lighter side of life has also been lit up in these past 50 years by some sportsmen and characters who would have graced any decade of Vincent's first century. After all, what does success in politics matter, as that earlier Vincent's Prime Minister, Lord Rosebery, more or less said, when compared to horse-racing? W B Woodgate himself loved the sport of kings. Rosebery won the Derby three times as an owner, twice while being Prime Minister for only fifteen months. C B Fry told his devoted biographer, Denzil Batchelor, on visiting stables in his 60s that he was thinking of taking up horse-racing. To which Batchelor replied: 'What as? Owner, trainer, jockey or horse?'

If the world was changing in March 1963, and by Larkin's account we could date the change as happening by 22 March when the Beatles released *Please, Please Me*, that was neatly in between Sharp's great try of Saturday 16 March and the Grand National of Saturday 30 March. There has been some extraordinary sports journalism by Vincent's men over 150 years, again following the example of Woodgate, the Club founder. But at least a place in the top three all-time Vincent's sports journalism awards could go to Lord Oaksey for his pioneering BBC television report, compiled in the days before the 1963 Grand National and shown in the run-up to the race itself. Vincent's has many distinguished family connections but the Oakseys rank high in this regard also. Lord Oaksey's father was the judge just mentioned as presiding over the Nuremburg trial as Lord Justice Lawrence, before becoming a Lord of Appeal. The extraordinary insight given to viewers in 1963 came from the invention that Woodgate had once prophesied, the helicopter. This was high-flying journalism of the highest class. Julian Wilson's obituary in the *Guardian* recalls Lord Oaksey's commentary from that helicopter view of the course four days before the National, a commentary which ended with the gift of prophecy: 'Round the last elbow into the straight … the final dregs of stamina are draining fast for horse and man alike. A hundred yards to go and perhaps another's head appears at his knee.'

If anything, it was bettered by an article written immediately after that same race and appearing the next day in the *Sunday Telegraph* of 31 March, again by Lord Oaksey, describing one of the most thrilling and agonising races, one to match on horseback Derek Johnson's silver medal in the 1956 Melbourne Olympics. What is more, Oaksey was himself the jockey who had led on Carrickbeg from the final fence until the last few strides when Ayala, at 66-1, won the day. Fry and Warner used to write about their own international cricket performances but this was accomplished with much grace amid great disappointment. Moreover, the race had followed the course shown and described by Oaksey in advance.

Three-quarters of a mile from home today the dream of a lifetime seemed to be becoming true before my eyes. 'Go on John, you'll win!' – the speaker, as I passed him before the second last, was Pat Buckley on Ayala. He thought it was true too. But half a minute later as Carrickbeg and I tired together in the final desperate 50 yards, it was he and Mr P B Raymond's gallant chestnut who dashed our hopes. ... then it happened – nothing much, invisible from the stands – but there 50 yards from home I felt Carrickbeg sprawl and change his legs. The rhythm was gone, and hard as I strove to pull him together, the last dreg of his stamina – and mine – had drained away. It still seemed possible – but then, like Nemesis, the worst sight I ever expect to see on a racecourse, Ayala's head appeared at my knee. He and Pat Buckley had never given up and must have struggled like heroes to make up four lengths from the last. But they did, and poor Carrickbeg, with no more help available from me, staggered home gasping, his job gallantly done, the prize so very nearly his ... it was all a marvellous, jumbled dream – a dream that only became a nightmare seconds before the dawn ...

As an amateur rider he had already won the Whitbread Gold Cup at Sandown and the Hennessy Gold Cup at Cheltenham on Taxidermist. He rode many more winners before retiring after a fall in 1975 but he was already involved in the media and in good causes. The year after his most famous outing in the Grand National, Lord Oaksey was a founder of the Brookshaw-Farrell Fund which became part of the Injured Jockeys' Fund. The jockeys Tim Brookshaw and Paddy Farrell had been paralysed when falling at Aintree. Under guidance from Lord Oaksey it has helped a thousand jockeys and their families. Oaksey himself fell in another National and was briefly unconscious, rallying to file his article for the *Sunday Telegraph* before going to hospital. It was not simply at Grand Nationals that Lord Oaksey wrote or rode or appeared on the BBC. He worked on television for over more than three decades, from the late 1960s until the beginning of this century, covering racing for ITV and Channel 4. He had studied law at Yale as well as Oxford and could easily have followed his father, and the founder of Vincent's, into the law but he much preferred to immerse himself in racing right up to his death in 2012 and especially to write, under such pen names as 'Hotspur' and 'Marlborough' in the *Daily Telegraph* and in the weekly Audax column in *Horse & Hound* magazine, for almost three decades. W B Woodgate would have approved.

If one man can span the entire half a century in horse-racing, another way of looking at Vincent's is to take a sport and race through some of the famous names of these 50 years. The idea that one of the showpiece varsity sports, rugby, was of poor quality after 1963 is not borne out by one of Oxford's most famous and infamous victories at the end of the 1960s. Tommy Bedford, the South Africa back row forward, had played in three varsity matches in 1965, 1966 and 1967, captaining the side in 1966, and he was vice-captain of the Springboks on their highly controversial tour in 1969. Chiefly remembered in the wider world for the anti-apartheid protests led by Peter Hain, subsequently a Labour government minister, the tour began with a game against Oxford on 5 November 1969 that was switched by the police from Iffley Road to Twickenham, in an attempt to protect the game from disruption. Oxford were captained by Chris Laidlaw, the outstanding New Zealand scrum-half, and included in the back row Peter Dixon. He was then a postgraduate in the middle of his sequence of four varsity matches from 1967 to 1970, including alongside Bedford in 1967, and who went on to captain England, play for the Lions on their victorious 1971 New Zealand tour and play against the All Blacks in the glorious Barbarians match in 1974. Dixon played for North-West Counties when they beat the All Blacks, captained by Ian Kirkpatrick, 16-14 at Workington on 22 November 1972, ending a losing streak of English sides (other than the national team) against the All Blacks of all 85 games since Vincent's 'Khaki' Roberts played in that game for Oxford in 1905.

Dixon was still beating the All Blacks, led by Graham Mourie, at the very end of the 1970s, when the North of England won 21-9 at Otley on 17 November 1979. Bedford did not play in the opening game of the 1969 tour which Oxford won 6-3, the same score by which Scotland, including Vincent's member Peter Stagg, beat the Springboks, captained for the day by Bedford. England also won, 11-8, captained by a Vincent's member, Bob Hiller, with Vincent's Nigel Starmer-Smith at scrum-half. Both Stagg and Hiller also toured with the Lions. Bedford is one of the former Springboks who has a good reputation in the new South Africa for having pressed change. South African, New Zealand and Australian rugby legends have continued to grace Iffley Road and Vincent's – Dugald and Donald Macdonald in the mid to late 1970s, Nick Mallett at the end of the decade, Phil Crowe in the early 80s, Ian Kirk, captain of the first team to win the World Cup in 1987; Brian Smith and Troy Coker of Australia also played for Oxford in the late 1980s. Joe Roff of Australia won the World Cup in 1999, playing also in the 1995 tournament and 2003 final, scoring in between times a famous interception try widely credited as the turning point of the Lions' 2001 tour of Australia. Roff captained Oxford as recently as 2007, having also played in 2006. Anton Oliver of New Zealand played in 2008. Roff returned to the varsity match in 2011 as touch judge and in 2012 as the main speaker at Vincent's eve-of-varsity dinner. Squarely in the middle of this sequence, England rugby stars Stuart Barnes, Simon Halliday and Victor Ubogu, and Ireland's Hugo MacNeill and Brendan Mullin all played for Oxford in the 1980s. Phil de Glanville played in the varsity match of 1990 and captained England later in the 90s. Even in 2012, the Vincent's president from 2006, and one of the fastest members of the Club of all time, Jonan Boto, has scored tries for and against the Barbarians who, like various club and national sides, have been coached by the aforementioned Nick Mallett. The Barbarians, as explained earlier, were given their motto by a Vincent's man from the 19th-century Blues teams and have included great Vincent's players throughout their history.

There are, then, exceptional individuals still drawn to Oxford's rugby union tradition. These are not simply good players, but some of the greatest in the game. Dugald Macdonald, for instance, from the 1970s would be in many selections of all-time greatest South African forwards. At scrum-half in your all-time world XV, Chris Laidlaw from the 1960s or David Kirk from the 1980s and 1990s would have a good claim. In the 1990s and in this century, Joe Roff has been selected in such all-time world's greatest teams. Nevertheless, in the new professional era of rugby union, where training is a full-time and well-rewarded occupation, the standard of Oxford's student teams as a whole cannot match that of the leading clubs. Oxford 2013 is not the same, in this respect, as Obolensky's Oxford in the 1930s, or Sharp's in the late 1950s and early 1960s. But Anton Oliver makes the point that it is also because rugby is itself an uncertain career, given injuries and the vagaries of form and selection, so he thinks that,

> You are not going to get any more All Blacks who are Rhodes Scholars in the future. My feeling is that if you are reasonably intelligent and you have got an inquiring mind, a professional rugby life is not enough now. It's a very uncertain path because of all sorts of things like injuries that you can't control.

There is still a pioneering spirit in the Club and the University, however, as illustrated by the leading light in Oxford's development of rugby league, Jon Hobart, a Vincent's member who has seen many rugby league Blues become members and some become presidents. Rugby players in either code have been prominent among recent Club officers and rugby league is not the only sport to have created new opportunities for Oxford Blues that were not there in Vincent's first 100 years. The presidents and other office-holders of Vincent's are also continuing to support their colleges, often playing in a variety of sports. So Jimmy Allan's Worcester might not have won rugby union Cuppers but they have won the college league and college Cuppers in football for season after season right up to 2013, helped by Adam Healy scoring goals for them while completing his doctorate in chemistry, with Blues in both rugby union and in the latest 2013 varsity soccer, and having served as secretary, treasurer and in 2012 president of Vincent's. With his pioneering research in energy, and his own energies in leadership on and off the sports pitches, it would be surprising if at Vincent's 200th anniversary, more had not been heard of Adam Healy. His successor, Jonathan Pearson-Stuttard, is not only a modern pentathlete and cross-country runner but another to have published already in academic journals, in his case on the unequal burden of coronary disease in the UK. The president in 2012–13, Ben Mansfield, is combining speaking at home and abroad for the Club as it approaches its anniversary with preparing for the refurbishment of the premises and being a doctoral researcher in science who rows for Oriel and sails for the University.

If it were ever true that only students in the arts could focus on sport, these three scientists have managed to balance demanding studies at all levels with their sports while holding high office in the Club. Hugh McCormick is the rugby-playing president of 2011 who had the wit to ask presidents of earlier generations to help put Vincent's on a business-like footing, as presidents were being dragged into too much daily administration. McCormick also had the vision to pioneer and promote Vincent's outreach scheme. A principal volunteer for those coaching sessions for school-pupils is Marcus-Alexander Neil, a rugby league Blue elected as president of Vincent's for 2013–14. This venture makes a difference by coaching local youngsters and encouraging them to aim high in their sport and their studies. Oxford undergraduates, including Vincent's members, helped in similar ways a century ago, but the revival of the practice is down to these individuals, backed by supportive Vincent's committees and alumni who have funded the projects. Both boys and girls are welcomed on summer camps and Atalanta's members coach alongside Vincent's men. Marcus-Alexander Neil spoke as president at the 150th anniversary Mansion House dinner, alongside Lord Patten, the Chancellor of the University, and Roger Gifford – the Lord Mayor of the City of London and another Vincent's member.

Both recent members and the youngsters they are inspiring come from a wide range of backgrounds. Nor were Vincent's characters from 1963 always from the most privileged of backgrounds. Stan Sanders, an African-American Rhodes Scholar and Vincent's member, threw the discus 52.62 metres in 1964, which stood as the Oxford record for almost all of this period, right up until 2008. Like Lord Oaksey, he went next to Yale Law School. In his case, he could have sought an Olympic place in the decathlon. He was being consistent in pursuing educational opportunities, as suggested more recently by Anton Oliver. Stan Sanders had preferred to come to Oxford rather than take up offers of professional American football. He later helped in his home city to organise the Los Angeles 1984 Olympics. He came from the Watts district of LA; his father was a garbage truck driver. His older brother, Ed, won Olympic gold in Helsinki 1952 in heavyweight boxing, beating Ingemar Johansson who went on to be the professional champion of the world. Ed left the navy to turn professional, was knocked out in the ring and died a few hours later. He had always encouraged Stan to study. One enduring lesson of these 50 years is that the high-flyers are taking off from all directions.

Vincent's British athletes and other sportsmen have also seen success in this era, starting with Adrian Metcalfe winning silver in the 4x400 relay in the Tokyo 1964 Olympics. David Hemery became an Oxford postgraduate student and Vincent's member in between winning three Olympic medals in two Games. Over Mexico 1968 and Munich 1972 he matched Bevil Rudd with the complete set of gold, silver and bronze. The silver came in the 4x400 in 1972, the bronze in the same Munich Games for the 400 metres hurdles. Like Jack Lovelock, Hemery had won gold with an Olympic and world record, in this case with a time of 48.12 for the 400 metres hurdles in Mexico 1968. Olympic medals from Vincent's could be multiplied, even by a single individual in the case of Sir Matthew Pinsent, but before coming to his extraordinary sequence, just one example of another Olympic champion from another country in another sport in the 70s would be

Two decades after the Abdication, former cricket Blue Walter Monckton (1891–1965) is seen with the Duke of Windsor, whom he advised during the 1935 crisis. (33)

Dr Robin Fletcher, 1952 Summer Olympics hockey medallist and, later, Warden of Rhodes House 1980–9. (34)

Pete Dawkins, Rhodes Scholar 1958, US College All Stars player, who introduced the torpedo pass (subsequently banned) to British rugby. (35)

Clive van Ryneveld, one of Vincent's great all-rounders, played rugby for Oxford and England from 1947 to 1949, before leading the South African cricket team in 19 Tests between 1951 and 1958. (36)

1928 Olympic gold medallist King Olav V of Norway with Queen Elizabeth II at a London polo match, 1959. (37)

Pope John XXIII hands a gold medal to Cardinal William Theodore Heard of Scotland to commemorate the 600th anniversary of the British College in Rome, June 1962. (38)

Left: In Vincent's centenary year, Vincent's member Richard Sharp introduces Prime Minister Harold Macmillan (Hon Member) to the England rugby team, 1963. (39)

Below: Colin Cowdrey walks out to bat with a broken arm, England v West Indies, Lord's, 25 June 1963. (40)

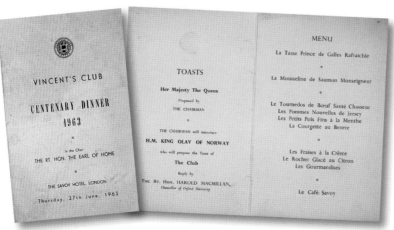

Above: Centenary Dinner menu, 1963. (41)

Left: The Nawab of Pataudi, dazzling stroke player, captain of Oxford and India. (42)

Right: Alec Douglas-Home (1903–95). As Lord Dunglass, played cricket for the University, and was president of Vincent's in 1926. Served as Prime Minister from October 1963 to October 1964, and joined the Lords as Baron Home of the Hirsel. (43)

The Beatles having a drink at Vincent's, 1964. (44)

Lord Oaksey (John Lawrence, 1929–2012), twice British Champion Amateur Jump Jockey (1957–8, 1970–1), racing journalist and commentator, who devoted over five decades to his sport. (45)

David Hemery, gold medallist in the 400m hurdles in the 1968 Olympics, Mexico City, and 1968 BBC Sports Personality of the Year. (46)

Far left: Chris Laidlaw, All Black international and later Rhodes Scholar, 1969. (47)

Left: Tommy Bedford, 1969 captain of the touring South African national rugby team and a fierce opponent of apartheid, who nevertheless encountered bitter protests on that tour. (48)

Left: New York Knicks player Bill Bradley was originally a member of the US gold medal basketball team at the 1964 Olympics. After taking up a Rhodes scholarship at Oxford (graduated 1968) he joined the Knicks and playing with them until his retirement in 1977, winning the NBA championships in 1970 and 1973. Later served three terms as a Democrat Senator for New Jersey. (49)

Right: Air Chief Marshal Sir Brian Burnett, photographed here in 1971. (50)

Norris McWhirter, co-founder of The Guinness Book of Records, *and timekeeper for Roger Bannister's record sub-four-minute mile, 6 May 1954. (51)*

J C Masterman (1891–1977), legendary sportsman, academic and World War Two spymaster. (52)

Captain Robert Nairac GC, pictured in Belfast,1977. He was murdered by the Provisional IRA later that year. (53)

Sir Rod Eddington, Vincent's president in 1977 and later CEO of British Airways. (54)

Colin Moynihan. Later Lord Moynihan, former Blue boat cox (1977), boxing Blue, British Olympic cox (1980), Minister of Sport (1987–90), voted BOA Chairman in 2005. (55)

Highly respected Oxford rowing coach Dan Topolski, in the year he published True Blue, the story of the 1987 Boat Race. (56)

Left: Donald MacDonald flourishes the award for the 133rd Boat Race, won by Oxford despite the withdrawal of US members. (57)

Right: David Kirk of New Zealand, the first captain to win the inaugural rugby World Cup in 1987, took up a Rhodes Scholarship in that year. (58)

Philip de Glanville, rugby Blue and later captain of England. (59)

Simon Halliday, rugby and cricket Blue 1979–82, played in 23 internationals from 1986 to 1992. (60)

Jeffrey (later Lord) Archer, athlete and best-selling author, whose Oxford career included introducing The Beatles to Vincent's bar. (61)

Sir Jeremy Greenstock, Rackets Blue and former UK ambassador to the UN, shortly after receiving his GCMG in 2004. (63)

A tribute in the Iffley Road pavilion to Katsuhiko Oku, the first Japanese national to play rugby for Oxford; he was tragically killed on diplomatic duty in Iraq in 2003. (62)

Left: New Zealander John Hood as Vice-Chancellor of Oxford University 2004–9. A Rhodes Scholar in 1977, he was squash and cricket Blue in that year. *(64)*

Right: Lord Butler, rugby Blue, president of Vincent's 1961–2. Private Secretary to five Prime Ministers, including Harold Wilson and Margaret Thatcher. Long-serving Chief Cabinet Secretary (1988–98), now Hon Life Chairman of the Club. *(65)*

Right: Craig Masback, CEO of US Track & Field 1997–2008. The 1980 US indoor mile champion, Masback ran 30 sub-four-minute miles. As a student at Oxford 1977–9 he ran his first sub-four-minute mile at the Iffley Road track, the second man after Roger Bannister to break the four-minute barrier. *(66)*

Below: Ian Ritchie, CEO of the Rugby Football Union, and formerly CEO of All England Lawn Tennis & Croquet Club, Wimbledon. *(67)*

Below right: Reg Clark, of Rhino Rugby. *(68)*

Malcolm Howard (centre) after stroking Oxford to victory in the 2013 Boat Race. He was a gold medallist for Canada in the 2008 Olympics and a silver medallist in London 2012. (69)

Davis Tarwater, US gold medallist swimmer at the 2012 London Olympics, graduated from St Antony's College in 2010. (70)

Sir Roger Gifford, Lord Mayor of London 2012–13, hosted the Vincent's 150th anniversary dinner in the Mansion House. (71)

Tony Abbott, a noted boxing Blue at Oxford, became Prime Minister of Australia in 2013, Vincent's 150th year. (72)

Marcus-Alexander Neil (president 2013–14) leads a Vincent's outreach team which holds sessions in the Iffley Road pavilion to enthuse young people to engage in sport and appreciate sporting values. (73)

Ave atque vale! *The main clubroom immediately before refurbishment, 2013. (74)*

Selwyn Maister's gold for New Zealand in hockey. In the 80s, the twin brothers Mark and Mike Evans won Olympic gold for Canada in the rowing eights in those Los Angeles 1984 Games, the victory which started Canada's stream of successes on the water and one which was in the balance as the home crew almost caught Canada. Holding off the USA to win Canada's first-ever Olympic gold at this event has had an impact on late 20th-century and early 21st-century Canadian rowing similar to the boost given to rowing in America by the Oxford-Harvard contest in the 19th century. Mark and Mike Evans had also rowed in the Boat Race in 1983 and returned in 1984, both years in winning crews. The first of these was the last of five Blues won by Boris Rankov.

Sir Matthew Pinsent began winning Olympic golds in Barcelona 1992 and continued in Atlanta 1996, Sydney 2000 and concluding, appropriately enough, in Athens 2004. Even so, and even though in his presidential year the Oxford Boat Race crew had another Barcelona 1992 gold medallist in the Canadian Bruce Robertson, Pinsent has written powerfully about the experience of losing to Cambridge. He later volunteered to help coach the women's crew and has continued to support varsity rowing, in 2012 as the assistant umpire (and spotting the saboteur in the water) and in 2013 becoming the umpire of the Boat Race.

Andy Triggs Hodge and Pete Reed won rowing gold in Beijing 2008 and London 2012. In 2005, St Catherine's were chasing Hertford but did not manage to bump them on the first three days of Eights Week, despite having Blues and international rowers in their boat, including Colin Smith, who went on to win an Olympic silver medal stroking the GB eight in Beijing 2008. On the Saturday, Andy Triggs Hodge flew back from winning gold in the world championships and came into the St Catz VIII which then did bump Hertford on the final day. He was studying for an MSc Water Science, Policy and Management. In urging potential donors to contribute to the Charles Wenden bursary fund at St Catherine's, he explained that

Sport is a key part of education. With the right balance and support it will not only improve academic work, but also the whole experience of a student's time at Oxford. It is so important that the enthusiasm of the students for sport is matched by the University as a whole: supported financially, and valued as a key part of education. If you're lucky enough to find a sport that is motivating, that has a great team atmosphere, and will endeavour to show you something that you didn't know about yourself before, you will be a richer person for it.

At each Olympiad, there is speculation that Oxford and Vincent's have ended their long winning streak. Yet time and again, an Olympian, or now a Paralympian, emerges from Oxford or decides, in the aftermath of their performance, to come to Oxford. Davis Tarwater won swimming gold in London 2012 as part of a USA relay squad. One of Vincent's new members in 2012, Daniel Hooker, a sprinter and long jumper, is aiming for the 2016 Rio Paralympics. Oxford's stroke in the 2013 Boat Race, Malcolm Howard, has already won gold for Canada in Beijing 2008, and switched to a new discipline to win silver in London 2012.

So Woodgate's own sport, rowing, continues to flourish. There have been times, however, when the traditions of the Boat Race have been questioned precisely because there are so many Olympian and world championship rowers coming from around the world, bringing different perspectives. Even at the end of the 1950s there had been a rebellion of sorts, with the war hero and double-gold Olympian 'Jumbo' Edwards having his coaching questioned, and the president of the OUBC, Ronnie Howard, having to assert himself against challenges from an American rower. In the middle of this period, Vincent's itself featured at a crucial moment in the Oxford Boat Race Mutiny of 1987. American rowers wanted one of their own, Chris Clark, to row instead of the president, Donald Macdonald, a mature Scottish student. Almost a decade earlier, Macdonald had rowed for Dan Topolski, Oxford's coach and himself a Blue rower and Vincent's member from the beginning of this period, at the London Rowing Club. He only came to higher education in his late 20s. He kept beating Clark in all the tests but the American rowers told the president that he should make way for the more experienced international oarsman. Macdonald's authority was shaken and he decided to reassert it by convening a meeting in Vincent's on 22 January. In his 1989 book *True Blue*, Dan Topolski makes Vincent's one of the characters in the drama:

> I walked alone into the club where lurks the history of Oxford's greatest sporting moments since the last century. I climbed the two flights of stairs into the big clubroom, with its deep sofas and chairs, its magazines and newspapers, and the aging permanence that dwells in such rooms. On days like this, when matters of

great moment are to be decided, the spirits of past glories seem strangely close, as if the ghosts of other sportsmen, from other times, who have also experienced turbulence and anger, are near ... All the rowing legends belonged to Vincent's; Davidge, Burnell, 'Jumbo' Edwards, Duncan Spencer and Ronnie Howard, and they had all sat in this room wrestling with the intricate problems of team selection, and the downfall of the traditional enemy one hundred and thirty miles away in Cambridge. None of them, however, had ever dealt with a more serious sporting quarrel than the one which now faced Donald and me.

The uprising was quelled, the Americans did not row; Macdonald drafted in members of the Isis crew and beat Cambridge. Even the book by Alison Gill, president of Oxford University Women's Boat Club in 1987, which is supportive of the Americans and critical of Macdonald and Topolski, recognises the aura of Vincent's for this meeting: 'They walked up the stairs past pictures of all the great Oxford sportsmen, and as they did so, no doubt memories of a few wild and raucous parties for which the club is famous crossed their minds!' That does not seem to follow but the scene is set nonetheless. It has been invaluable over 150 years to have a place, established and maintained by students, that doubles as a venue for socialising and for determining matters of sporting life and death.

Win or lose, within one's own team or against Cambridge, it is easy to see how such experiences of strong wills, discord and the need to rebuild are thought to be formative for high-flyers in life beyond sport, especially in business. Sir Rod Eddington was Vincent's president in 1977, having come to Pembroke from Western Australia as a Rhodes Scholar in 1974. He gained a doctorate in engineering and played cricket for Oxford. Joining Cathay Pacific after Oxford and later becoming CEO of British Airways from 2000 to 2005, his business career has naturally been written about extensively in the media under headlines such as 'High-flyer'. At British Airways, he took some popular decisions, such as abandoning the abstract tail-fin designs introduced by his predecessor Robert Ayling that had so irritated Margaret Thatcher, restoring the traditional Union Jack, and some unpopular ones, such as stopping Concorde. His major success was in keeping the company flying high in the aftermath of the 9/11 attacks on America in 2001, which had calamitous effects on some other international airlines. Knighted for his services to aviation, and the author of a major report into transport for the government here, and another one for the government in Victoria, he has since leaving British Airways held various non-executive appointments, including board positions with four of the world's major private sector businesses, Rio Tinto Zinc, News Corps, JP Morgan and the parent company of Cathay, John Swire. He has taken particular pleasure in chairing the body bringing major sporting events to Melbourne in particular and Victoria in general. With his presidency of Vincent's and the success of Melbourne in turning around its fortunes through its sports and major events strategy, Sir Rod is also asked regularly by business and sporting journalists about the relationship between the two spheres of life. He agrees that there are common elements:

> … sport is a well-established metaphor for business and vice versa. There is something very frank about the assessment of performance on the sports field that translates precisely to business. Sport is all about preparation, clarity of thought, having an effective game plan and demonstrating the ability to cope with adversity. These are all important qualities in business.

Dr John Hood came to Worcester as a Rhodes Scholar in 1976, already with a doctorate in engineering from New Zealand. He studied for a Masters in management, played squash for Oxford against Cambridge and also played cricket for the University, becoming a member of Vincent's. His subsequent business career in New Zealand has been described as 'stellar', which is as high-flying as journalism gets. He then became Vice-Chancellor of the University of Auckland, restoring its fortunes, before becoming the first Vice-Chancellor in the 800-year history of Oxford to be appointed from outside the ranks of current heads of house. He followed Sir Colin Lucas, the distinguished historian and another Vincent's member. In his five-year term, from 2004 to 2009, he set the foundations for the Oxford Thinking appeal which has now raised over £1 billion. He challenged Oxford to reform its governance, meeting opposition but not fighting shy of controversy. He now has a portfolio of roles as the chairman of industrial and educational organisations, including chairing the board of the Rhodes Trust and serving on the board of the Mandela Rhodes Foundation alongside one of South Africa's most successful businessmen, Julian Ogilvie Thompson, a Rhodes Scholar, who joined Anglo American Corporation, which became Anglo American plc.

Each generation yields more high-flyers in finance, business and academe. It comes as no surprise that the Evans brothers have proceeded to high-flying business careers, and it is not only Olympic champions among Vincent's members who will make their way to the highest echelons of a Goldman Sachs or other bank or private equity firm or hedge fund. Almost all of these characters are, without making a fuss, philanthropists. The Luddington Prize for Outstanding Academic and Sporting Achievement, for example, gives £500 to every St Edmund Hall student who achieves a First and a Blue. The fund was endowed by Vincent's Richard Luddington, now a leading banker, who won Blues in the late 70s and early 80s in Rugby, Hockey and Cricket while gaining First Class Honours in History and then a Masters in management. So his old college is now awarding his prize for such combinations as 'a first in Biochemistry and a Blue in Sailing' or 'a first in Engineering and Blues in Athletics, Swimming and Modern Pentathlon', together with such doubles as Law and Karate, Earth Sciences and Rowing, and Geography and Lacrosse.

Not many of these busy leaders in banking or business want the bureaucracy that nowadays goes with the UK's quangos and other public bodies, but some are prepared to come into the public eye to serve a business, sporting, cultural, charitable or other good cause, usually in a non-executive leadership role. For example, becoming chair of the governors of the BBC, or now of the BBC Trust, is regarded as a mark of a high-flyer. From 1986 to 1996, the chairman was Marmaduke Hussey, a Vincent's man featured in the previous chapter. He was succeeded by Sir Christopher Bland, another Vincent's member, who served until 2001. Christopher Bland fenced for Oxford and for Ireland in the Rome 1960 Olympics, also leading Oxford's modern pentathlon club. He has chaired many business, cultural and health organisations such as London Weekend TV, the BBC, BT and the Royal Shakespeare Company, publishing firms and the Leith School of Food and Wine. The current chairman, Lord (Chris) Patten is both Chancellor of the University of Oxford and now an Honorary Member of Vincent's, having played rugby for Balliol with Richard Sharp.

At a Vincent's gathering to celebrate the 150th anniversary, other captains, often knights, of industry could include Sir Christopher Hogg, who served as a paratrooper, worked for the Hill Samuel bank at the start of this period in 1963, ran Courtaulds from the late 70s to mid-90s and has taken on various roles in finance and business, including chairing GlaxoSmithKline, Reuters and Allied Domecq, or Sir Christopher Wates of the leading construction company that bears his family name, or David Veit, an Olympian hockey player for Great Britain whose business career on the other side of the Atlantic has included Pearson, Bain, Carnco and the American Stock Exchange. Likewise, there are other leaders of the UK's cultural assets, beyond the BBC, such as Lord (Peter) Palumbo, who has chaired the Arts Council, served as a trustee of the Tate and the National History Museum and is now chairing the Serpentine Gallery, as well as engaging in property development and being a patron of the arts in many guises.

If these seem like very British or Anglo-American careers, the examples of Eddington and Hood criss-crossing the world are a counterbalance and the globetrotting of Craig Masback is even more closely related to sport. The Achilles Club is a wonderful institution, uniting Oxford and Cambridge athletes and setting the gold standard for all sports in meticulous record-keeping. Its annual report is a gold-medal mine of varsity rivals developing friendships and broadening their horizons. For example, 25 years after the 1978 Achilles tour of Australia and Singapore, Steve White recalled that the bargain price for travelling around the world attracted a strong team which had 'two athletes of exceptional class in Craig Masback and Julian Goater'. He jokes that, 'We were the Qantas Achilles team. It said so on our tracksuits. The airline had given us free flights. We had Tommy Macpherson to thank for negotiating that and other deals which left us paying no more than the token, bargain basement price. As the trip progressed, tracksuit tops were swapped and so our visibly unanimous endorsement of Qantas gradually dissolved.' Tommy Macpherson is the Vincent's member and Achilles life president mentioned in the previous chapter for his exploits as a war hero.

Craig Masback has himself written for the Achilles Club about his experience of coming to Oxbridge from

[an] American college athletics experience featuring multiple full-time coaches, free training and competitive shoes, daily laundering of my workout clothes, nicely pressed competitive uniforms, and free travel to competitions. Imagine my shock at an Oxford world of no team practices, key decisions made by fellow students, and uniforms and travel to competitions 'at cost'.

Masback was a serious athlete, not only securing his Blue and achieving a double victory in 800 and 1500 metre varsity races but adapting also to cross-country. He reports that he ran his 'first sub-four-minute mile at Iffley Road in June of 1978 in a match with Penn and Cornell (a race attended by Sir Roger who was there to honour the groundskeeper who had prepared the track on the historic day in May of 1954)'. This was in fact the first time since that famous day that anyone had run a sub-four-minute mile at Iffley Road. Craig Masback improved his personal best for the mile the following year, running the 1979 Golden Mile in 3:52.02, and became the Chief Executive of US Track & Field, the governing body of athletics in the USA.

Masback came to love the Oxford sporting ethos: 'As other traditional sports events have sacrificed their essence and distinctiveness in a pursuit for sports marketing dollars and media attention, the Varsity Match and Achilles Tours remain true to their origins, giving those of us lucky enough to have experienced them cherished lifelong memories.' It would be good to know whether he kept or swapped his Qantas kit, as Craig Masback left US Track & Field a few years ago to become the Director for Business Affairs of Nike Global Sports Marketing Division. Nike are now taking on the mantle of supplying kit to all Oxford University sports teams. Reg Clark's Rhino company, as we have seen, is one of their competitors with a record of supporting Oxford and all levels of sport. Masback and Clark are pioneers of the opportunities in recent decades of sport as an industry.

There are many other ways, however, of combining a career with a love of sport. From Vincent's in the 1960s, and from the Oxford Union where he was president, the Hon Michael Beloff QC has become the pioneer of sports law, its major authority and the doyen of Olympic appeal judges. As president of Trinity for a decade, he returned to the track to gain points for his adopted college and as a benefactor he was one of those Heads of House who donated not only his time and talents but even a new boat. From the 1970s, Ian Ritchie's high-flying career at the highest echelons of sport has included a spell at Wimbledon, where as chief executive of the All England Club he was responsible for the £100 million retractable roof, and now at Twickenham, where he is the chief executive of the Rugby Football Union, the sport's governing body in England.

In the 1970s, a Vincent's cricketer from the 1950s, Abdul Kardar, an all-rounder, chaired the Pakistan Cricket Board, having earlier played for the University, India and then for Pakistan, captaining them to victories against every country they played against. Imran Khan and others regard Kardar as the father of Pakistani cricket. Kardar was highly rated by his Oxford team-mate Colin Cowdrey and explained that his own inspiration was a Vincent's member from an earlier generation of colonial administrators, Sir George Abell, whom he saw playing at the Lahore Gymkhana and whose inspiration led Kardar to Oxford. Sir George Abell was the Richard Luddington of his generation, securing Blues in rugby, cricket and a First in Greats, captaining the University in rugby and returning from Asia to high office in the Bank of England, and as chairman of the Rhodes trustees.

Also in the 1970s, a Vincent's member from the 1920s became the chairman of the Football Association. Professor Sir Harold Thompson, well known as a research scientist in the war and as the founder of the Pegasus football club for Oxbridge alumni, had already become a figure of controversy for sacking Sir Alf Ramsey as England's manager. Meanwhile, Oxford cricket in the mid to late 70s remained strong, with the Kent and England batsman Chris Tavare to the fore and Vic Marks, the Somerset all-rounder, captaining Oxford for two seasons and also gaining hockey Blues. Tavare went on to a career in teaching, while Marks has become one of the country's leading sports journalists. A Vincent's member, law student and rugby blue from the 1980s, Richard Glynn, pioneered new approaches to betting with Sporting Index and is now the chief executive of Ladbroke's, the leading bookmaker. Again, W B Woodgate would have been delighted.

For those who want to break away from sport in their working lives, the lure of the big companies has perhaps faded. In many ways, the excitement of the economy has moved to the start-ups that spin out of academia, and today's graduates are much more likely to be entrepreneurs starting their own business than the heirs of an already established organisation such as Nike. Colin Smith, for example, came from Zimbabwe to study at Oxford and row for the University. He won silver as stroke of the Great Britain eight at Beijing 2008 and returned to study for his MBA at the Said Business School in Oxford while being president of OUBC. He has set up his own company. Many science students and researchers wish to combine their academic work with pursuing commercial applications. A recent head of Chemistry at Oxford, Professor Graham Richards, relates the story in his memoir, *50 Years at Oxford*, of discussing a University spin-out, worth £20 million, with the chairman of a London stockbroking firm: 'The discussion did not start very encouragingly … but a chance twist in the conversation changed everything. He asked if the tie which I happened to be wearing was a Vincent's Club tie. I replied that it was indeed and we started to converse about sport … The whole atmosphere changed. The deal was done …'. It is not enough, of course, to have a symbol of membership of Vincent's if the underlying substance of a business proposition does not merit such support, but the point is rather about atmosphere. The reputation of Vincent's at its best is taken, on this approach, to suggest a hinterland, a sense of balance, an understanding of intense competitiveness and yet wholehearted team spirit.

There are still Vincent's members who want to explore the heights and depths of the world, in the spirit of Sandy Irvine, Wilfred Thesiger and other pioneers of adventure. Sundeep Dhillon, for example, read Medicine in the late 1980s and early 1990s, chairing the Oxford University Exploration Club and leading a research expedition to Mt Kanchenjunga, the third highest mountain in the world. By 1996, he was close to the summit of Everest when the weather prevented him reaching the summit and claimed the life of another climber. In 1998, he was back to break the world record, by becoming the youngest person to climb the highest mountains on all seven continents. He has been the first to climb peaks in Antarctica.

And there are members of Vincent's who follow a vocation that seems even more of a mystery to those who would only judge success in terms of commerce or public recognition, such as Fr Felix Stephens OSB, a Benedictine monk of Ampleforth, who recently returned to Oxford to serve as Master of St Benet's Hall some 40 years after he combined his studies there with membership of Vincent's and being secretary of the Oxford University Cricket Club, in which capacity he reinvigorated cricket Cuppers. Once more however, it is evident that the sermon-writing founder of Vincent's, W B Woodgate, would have understood Fr Felix's commitment to the church, to inter-college competition and to being an outstanding Head of House, even though cricket was not the founder's idea of sport. Revd Nick Stacey, one of the heroes of the last chapter, became in this era well known as a radical churchman engaged in social action. Revd Andrew Wingfield Digby, a cricket Blue, is one of the pioneers of sports chaplaincy, from the Olympics to the England cricket team.

Woodgate would also have recognised, and been amused by, the way in which the Club 145 years after he founded it continued to bemuse but attract scholar athletes from all over the world through its atmosphere. Writing in the *New York Times* in 2008, Stephen Danley, a newcomer to Oxford, who had played basketball at the highest levels of American college sport, tried to explain the Club in less august terms than James Morris had in 1965. After a game for the University,

> The festivities took place at Vincent's Club. Vinnie's is pure Oxford. It has a dress code and pictures of old students all over the walls ... Vincent's Club is old school. At lunch-time it is an all-male eating club, and the process of becoming a member is shrouded in mystery. You have to be invited to join, but asking how you receive an invitation is a disqualifier.
>
> On Wednesday nights, Vinnie's becomes the postmatch gathering place; all Oxford sports play on Wednesdays. Teams gather there for the drinks. The bar serves the appropriate winter ales and mixed drinks, but has specials called pinkies and perkies. A pinky is grapefruit juice, orange juice and five shots of gin. A perky is grapefruit juice, lemonade and five shots of vodka. I can attest firsthand that perkies have the power to turn a couple of postmatch games into an ill-advised Wednesday night introduction to the Euro club scene.

High spirits are certainly part of the Vincent's experience for many but there is also a quieter way of concluding this sketch of the Club's membership from its 100th to its 150th years. This is an echo of Alec Douglas-Home knowing which way the wind blows and of Sir Edward Grey writing about and practising the art of fishing. In May 1984, a great Vincent's all-rounder became the world champion in the third sport for which he was renowned, at the age of 63. Tony Pawson had played cricket for Kent and made his football debut for Charlton Athletic in the Boxing Day game in 1951, beating and scoring against Tottenham Hotspur. He died in 2012 at the age of 91 after a career in industry, as a personnel director for Reed International, with a sideline in sporting journalism, writing principally about cricket and football for *The Observer*. A double Blue at cricket and football, he made a century on his debut for Oxford, against Gloucestershire, and later became one of many Vincent's members to have scored 150 in a first-class innings, against Worcestershire. He was selected for the Great Britain football squad at the London 1948 Olympics, although he did not get a game, and in 1978 he was selected for the England fly-fishing team, becoming in 1984, in Spain, the first

Englishman to win the individual World Fly Fishing championship, at the age of 63. He had been mentioned in dispatches when on active service in Italy and North Africa, defusing landmines. He played football in the army with Tom Finney, whom he taught to fish and from whom he learned a great deal about soccer. Pawson won the FA Amateur Cup twice with Pegasus, the combined Oxford and Cambridge club, in 1950 and 1953. In the late 1940s he had captained an Oxford cricket team that included two future Test captains, in Abdul Kardar of Pakistan and Clive van Ryneveld of South Africa. In his 50s, he returned to the Parks in the 1970s to score 46 against an Oxford attack that was led by Imran Khan, another future Pakistan Test captain.

Pawson's father, also at Christ Church, had played football for Oxford before the First World War. After the Second World War, Tony Pawson tells us that, 'Among the outside lecturers to quicken the imagination was J C Masterman, Provost of Worcester, writer of detective novels and a perceptive watcher in the Parks, always ready with sensible advice and kindly encouragement'. In 1988 Pawson was appointed OBE for his contributions to improving access for anglers with disabilities. Obituaries, including from Vic Marks, one of his successors at *The Observer*, are unanimous in praising him as a sportsman, a gentleman and a gentle man. In 2012, the Club of Woodgate, Buchan, Grey, Douglas-Home and many other sportsmen who enjoyed country pursuits, could take a quiet pride in an obituary from outside the noisier world of pinkies and perkies. Woodgate especially, having written for decades as a journalist, would have appreciated Pawson's own talents as a journalist and the fact that *Trout Fisherman* published this tribute from Bob Church:

> Tony Pawson was a much-loved sportsman. He had played football and cricket at the highest level, but it is for his contribution to fly-fishing for trout he was best known. In 1984 I qualified for England to fish in Spain along with Tony, he was elected captain. Tony was the perfect gentleman but also had a very competitive streak. It was clear to me England had the right captain in Tony. We were to fish the River Tormes in Salamanca. Going to Spain a week before the competition day gave us time to practise, the river was running high from flood. Instead of the usual dry fly method, Tony and the team opted to use slow sink lines and traditional English fly patterns such as the Black & Peacock Spider. Casting to the centre of

the river and allowing the current to swing the flies into your downstream bank and slow figure-of-eight retrieve. We stuck to Tony's decision and it worked. Tony won the whole event. Tony was the new World Fly Fishing individual champion and we as his team were a close runner up as second. So it was gold for Tony and silver for the team. Tony was presented with the largest trophy I had ever seen.

As Vincent's celebrated its 150th anniversary through a major refurbishment which required taking down the pictures, indeed closing the premises for a few months, there was time to consider which trophies and other memorabilia, as well as which pictures, to reinstate and how to reflect the balance between tradition and change. As this chapter has sought to demonstrate, Club members have continued in this third half-century from 1963 to 2013 to achieve great things, on and off the sports fields and rivers of the world, with innumerable high-flyers in many spheres, still playing sport half a century or more after their election to Vincent's.

In the few months between the 150th anniversary and this book going to press, this is illustrated by the innumerable handsome tributes to Vincent's members who have died in the 2013–14 academic year. Jonathan 'Pom Pom' Fellows-Smith died on 28 September 2013, aged 81, and was mourned in tennis as well as cricket and rugby circles, with tales of his senior tennis victories in recent years. When the president from the centenary year, Joe McPartlin, died on 24 October 2013 aged 75, *The Scotsman* said he 'played rugby with a smile on his face', was 'elected president of the exclusive Vincent's Club, which was limited to 150 members, for outstanding Oxford University sportsmen' and 'never really left Oxford' but enjoyed life as a talented teacher and after-dinner speaker. When Sir Christopher Chataway died on 19 January 2014, aged 82, obituaries recorded that among his many high-flying achievements in sport, the media, industry, politics and wider public service, he ran the Great North Run half-marathon, at an impressive pace, in his seventies for the Vicky's Water charity. David Cameron, the Prime Minister, said that, 'Chris was one of a kind; throwing himself into every project and achieving so much in so many fields…'.

CHAPTER 5

Against the Current?
Vincent's and the Future

Oxford's Pitt Rivers Museum introduces its archive of 38,000 photographic negatives by declaring that the photographer and benefactor 'Sir Wilfred Thesiger (1910–2003) was probably the greatest traveller of the twentieth century, and one of its greatest explorers'. There is always another pioneer, hero and high-flyer among Vincent's alumni who could have been included in earlier chapters – or indeed already is the subject of whole books. Thesiger was a member of Vincent's, a boxing Blue and captain of the University boxing club. He joined the SAS within weeks of the death of fellow Vincent's member and SAS co-founder Jock Lewes. He is a prime example of the unconventional Vincent's sportsman who has the courage to stand against the current. This is not the same, however, as saying that the current drift is always wrong or that the past was always better. What Thesiger reports in new editions of *Arabian Sands* of returning to Oman and Abu Dhabi after more than a quarter of a century, and then again after almost as long an interval, might be said of any alumnus on returning to any university or sporting club. When he went back in 1977, he was 'disappointed and resentful' of the changes since he had left in 1950. When he next visited, in 1990, however, he was 'reconciled to the inevitable changes' and 'deeply impressed by the warmth of the welcome and the overwhelming hospitality'.

In this 150th anniversary year, Vincent's is modernising its premises. Some will fear that the Club risks thereby losing something of the aura described by Morris, Cowdrey, Swanton et al, but should in time be reconciled to such necessary improvements, generously funded by a few alumni, as making the upper-floor locations fully accessible to all members and guests with disabilities. Beyond the physical setting of the Club, some Oxford alumni regret what they see as the passing of their particular sporting era. Over half a century, however, what seems initially challenging can come to be regarded as inevitable and even desirable, albeit different. There is much talk nowadays of 'scholar athletes', and the diversity of having over 80 sports played at University level is an indication of a continuing commitment to a well-rounded student experience.

Can any grand conclusions be drawn from these vignettes of Vincent's members over the Club's first century and a half? When John Buchan in 1898 wrote a history of Brasenose, his own college and W B Woodgate's, he explained that, 'The book is in no sense a minute history; rather it is an attempt to cast a rather bald material into narrative form'. In fact, Brasenose has plenty of records of its sporting and other prowess. Vincent's, however, does not. Buchan noted in his conclusion that, 'in bringing a sketch of a college's history to a close, it is the habit of historians to embark on theories of college character and college spirit'. He eschewed that temptation. The ethos of a Club is even more ethereal, especially one which has for much of its 150 years kept its records to the absolute minimum – and then lost them or hidden them in an attic.

In this case, the choice of narrative has already indicated some broad themes, of pioneers, heroes and high-flyers. Since Woodgate was founding a club for all-rounders, it is at once obvious that this division is artificial, as is the division into half-centuries. Individuals span those divides, both of the themes and the ages. There are so many characters among the membership that no introduction to this extraordinary network of scholar-athletes could satisfy readers that the few examples cited of pioneers, heroes or high-flyers are the best ones or that these are the right categories. There are Prime Ministers who have not even been mentioned so far. Sir John Gorton described himself as having 'majored in rowing' at Woodgate's own college, Brasenose, in the 1930s, before his heroics as a pilot in the second world war and his controversial arrival and departure as Prime Minister of Australia. He was a member of Vincent's. Woodgate has a lesson from rowing for other politicians and perhaps for those who are over-ambitious in their estimation of their own talents:

> I have in my time known many a man who made an excellent No 7 or No 6; but who had the misfortune to demoralize an eight if he essayed to row stroke to it. Balfour is an analogy with this situation.

In Woodgate's own sport of rowing, there are many Olympic champions, such as the father-and-son gold-medal winners Charles and Dickie Burnell, who have not featured, partly because the well-documented sports have told their own stories so well. Vincent's great golfer, Cyril Tolley, has likewise been omitted, as the literature of golf is replete with stories of his prowess. He even pops up as a line judge in one of the most controversial games of women's tennis in history. He had won the Military

Cross in the First World War. In a famous case, he sued when he believed that C B Fry's family, the chocolate makers, could have compromised his amateur status as a golfer by using his image without permission for an advertisement. The very fact that he was well known enough for Fry's to have drawn on the public appreciation of him shows the impact he had. Cyril Tolley, having insisted on his amateurism and yet given the law a nudge towards the modern professional focus on image rights, continued to serve sport out of the limelight. In his 80s, he was still president of the golf club he had joined almost 70 years earlier as a junior member, Eastbourne Downs. Tolley's second sport of tennis is similarly well served at the highest national levels by Vincent's men. In addition to having Ian Ritchie as its chief executive at Wimbledon in recent years, tennis has transformed itself in recent decades under three long-serving chairmen of the All England Lawn Tennis Club who are Vincent's men, the late Air Vice-Marshal, Sir Brian Burnett, also a war hero, John Curry and Tim Phillips, both CBE in recognition of their service to the sport.

The Guardian did well to spot the Trinity College, Oxford, connection but missed the fellowship of Vincent's when it noted in 2007 that Ian Ritchie and Etienne de Villiers, then the chairman of the Association of Tennis Professionals, played a major part in bringing the World Tour final to London for 2009 to 2012. As already explained, Ritchie has moved on to masterminding not only the running of domestic rugby at Twickenham but the major business of the 2015 rugby union World Cup. De Villiers, originally from South Africa and a Rhodes Scholar with a business background from McKinsey to Disney, private equity and chairing the BBC's commercial arm, has played a significant part in other sporting ventures from Formula 1 to providing at short notice the setting for the Indian Premier League to launch its Twenty20 format in South Africa. There are other models of Vincent's members working in the massive sports business sector. Guy Kinnings, for example, graduated in law and worked in a City law firm but has since spent twenty years in the same world-leading sports business, IMG, where he is now the global head of golf. Ivan Gazidis similarly has specialised in a single sport. Of Greek descent, his father Costa Gazidis was a doctor and ANC member imprisoned in South Africa. Ivan went to school in England and studied Law at St Edmund Hall, winning Blues in football. He was with Major League Soccer's management team from its beginning in 1994 until as Deputy Commissioner, he was head-hunted by Arsenal to become their chief executive in 2009. Another career path altogether has been pursued by Chris Jenkins, a cox in his undergraduate days and for Wales when rowing was a Commonwealth sport, who has steadfastly worked for Welsh rowing and then for Wales across a range of sports as the country prepares for the Glasgow 2014 Commonwealth Games. From a supreme sportsman such as Tolley serving as a local club officer in his retirement, through to Jenkins serving his country by supporting athletes with little funding, through to Kinnings and Gazidis handling deals each worth tens of millions of pounds or de Villiers ranging across several sports or Ritchie leading the governance and main business venture in two sports, Vincent's members are influential in sport at every level. It is not simply that Vincent's offers an unrivalled network but that it is making a difference in such a major aspect of lives all over the world. Sport has become a major business. The figure of £500 billion is regularly quoted to illustrate the scale of the global sport industry but the excitement it brings to players and followers of sport all over the world is priceless, as is the expertise in world-class performance which the Vincent's network can bring back to Oxford.

There is a great resource here for current members who can draw on the wisdom of former members. A conversation with living presidents of the 1960s might well help their counterparts 50 years later – sailing's Ben Mansfield (2012–13) and rugby league's Marcus-Alexander Neil (2013–14) – in addressing the challenges and opportunities facing the Club. Each, of course, has other sporting interests and almost all Vincent's members mix participating, spectating and volunteering at different levels in different sports at different times. The conversation might, for example, be on a towpath or over a game of golf. Brian Burnett once gave a speech in honour of J C Masterman at a Wimbledon dinner where he recalled the fun they had playing squash competitively against each other. And there are always Vincent's presidents of an earlier era who are still playing another sport at the very highest competitive levels. John Webster, president in 1979, captained Great Britain to its 2011 Palma World Championship title in rifle shooting. On setting out for Australia on that occasion, he explained that he had experience of playing rugby 'in Oxford front rows in the early 1980s with Bill Ross, Queensland Red and Wallaby international, and Tony Abbott, now leader of the Opposition in Australia' but thought that rifle tours to Australia were special for more than that: 'the banter, the camaraderie, the rivalry, the history and, above all perhaps, the welcome.' This encapsulates the Woodgate doctrine of 'sport, sympathy and sincerity'. The late Joe McPartlin, who played rugby for Teddy Hall social side Hilarians on the Wednesday and Scotland v Wales on the Saturday, wrote about the relative disasters of losing an international and a Cuppers game. He had many sporting triumphs to celebrate but, self-effacingly, he recalled of 1963: 'Pure nepotism among Hall members got me elected president of Vincent's, and as it was the centenary year I had to sit with the celebrities at the Savoy dinner. It was a relief to discover that King Olav spoke perfect English.'

From the most serious to the most carefree of times, a sense of friendship, humour and not taking rules or themselves too seriously has often surfaced in the stories of Vincent's. When W B Woodgate quoted a newspaper commenting on 'Woodgate's heroic conduct' it was about his beloved younger brother, General Sir Edward Woodgate, who was killed in action in South Africa. He was impressed with his brother's robust insight, which will be appreciated by many Vincent's members from South Africa and beyond, that, 'If you want to be pals with a Boer, pick a quarrel, punch his head, and he's your friend'.

W B himself was always ready to help a friend in need. When the Vincent's president of 1869, S H 'Wangy' Woodhouse, wanted a ticket to the boat race dinner in 1874, 'the last year that UBC crews dined at Mansion House', Woodgate said Woodhouse could have his ticket as he was going instead to see a rower who was ill, and then helped Woodhouse in what he called an 'aquatic forgery' by altering the ending of the surname on the card. We can take it from this that Woodgate would have been amused if that 150th anniversary dinner of Vincent's at the Mansion House had been Woodgate-crashed.

Did the founder go to Vincent's much himself? J C Masterman recalled that Woodgate did turn up at the Club from time to time in Masterman's undergraduate days, just before the First World War. In Woodgate's own reminiscences, written in 1910, there is only one incident where there is even a tangential example of Woodgate referring to making use of the Club's facilities, namely the (famously free) stationery of its early years. When Alfred Chichele Plowden, later a magistrate, was a student and had broken a street lamp, he had taken refuge from the University police in another student's lodgings. Woodgate willingly swapped clothes, wandered out as a decoy and allowed Plowden to escape to college in time for the midnight curfew. Woodgate had given his name and address and was expecting a summons from the proctor. When none came, Woodgate went to the proctor, interrupting his lecture to assure him that the police had got the wrong man. The proctor was perfectly willing to believe Woodgate but mystified as to why he should have been summoned by an undergraduate from his own lecture to be told his version of an escapade that had not otherwise been brought to his attention. So 'I retired, shamefaced; and sent Furneaux a line of apology from Vincent's, for the intrusion'.

Mysteries remain. One speculative solution to the question why Woodgate did not establish the Club until the very end of his undergraduate days and did not seem to base himself there very much afterwards, despite being a frequent visitor to Oxford, is that perhaps he suffered from a mild form of claustrophobia. It would be prying to seek to solve other mysteries about the founder. His obituaries concluded with the classic formula that, 'He never married' or 'He was unmarried', 'a lifelong bachelor' or 'a confirmed bachelor'. Sir Theodore Cook, his editor at *The Field*, belabours the point, saying in an otherwise splendid encomium that Woodgate would never tell him why he never married. Why should he? We can take it from this that, as Woodgate did not want to discuss his private life with his contemporaries and did not refer to it in 500 pages of his own reminiscences, he would not want any more to be said about what the obituaries called his Bohemian lifestyle in an account of the club he founded.

In the opening chapter, some sense was given of the impact of his death. In conclusion, it is worth returning to the lessons in his death for the Club. Another great rower wrote a definitive letter to *The Field*, published on 20 November 1920, about Woodgate's founding of Vincent's:

> The club was certainly originated by my old friend Woodgate … Early in 1863 Woodgate told me that he had the offer of the rooms over Vincent's library, exactly opposite All Souls, and meant to establish a club there for the best hundred men at Oxford, and asked me to co-operate with him in making out the list. He did not propose to invite any man who had not made, or was not making, his mark as a good sportsman – or who was not socially desirable … On a visit to Oxford almost twenty-five years ago I was surprised to find the club had migrated to other quarters, but still keeping the name of Vincent's, and apparently still popular.
>
> Frank Harcourt Gooch. (Formerly of Merton College.)

Woodgate himself had explained that 'Running water ever had fascination for me, whether brook or flood. I can look for hours on a running river, and read sermons in it. More especially Henley Bridge at night-time has a weird fascination for me', a fascination which some obituarists linked to the classic Greek myths about death. Two years before the birth of W B, his father had given the prestigious Bampton Lectures in the University of Oxford. Canon Henry Woodgate dedicated these 1838 lectures, when published the following year, to his friend, John Henry Newman. Woodgate senior began with salutary words for an enduring Club:

> It is the lot of all institutions administered by human agency, that in their passage through the hands of men, they have a tendency to deteriorate; and this, not so much in themselves and in their own nature, as by departing from their original principles, and thus becoming corrupted. Hence it becomes necessary, from time to time, to return to their original principle and purpose, to compare their present state with their first design, their practice with their theory. To this, all institutions incorporated on human society are liable, whatever their origin, whether human or divine; our natural tendency is to gravitate, to sink from the point at which we set out on any moral course. In peaceable times, we are more especially prone to this; we are apt to lose sight, partially or entirely, of the principle on which the institution of which we are members was originally based; and then it is, that on looking back, and comparing our principle with our practice, we discover, perhaps for the first time, how far we have deviated from it.

Woodgate senior was talking about the church, of course, but his words apply to a club of such longevity as Vincent's. The Bampton lecturer put the point about continuity well in observing that, 'Others have laboured, and we have entered into their labours; and, by the same appointment, we must be content to labour, though others shall enter into it and reap its fruits'.

The Field could hardly cope with the reaction to Woodgate's death. He died on All Saints' Day, 1 November 1920. So the edition of 6 November gives his obituary. The 13 November edition reports on his funeral:

> The first part of the service was conducted in Henley Parish Church with the simplest possible rites, and then all moved away along that beautiful highway out of the town called the Fair Mile to the cemetery on the slope of the hill, where the road forks to Nettlebed on the left and on the right to Hambleden. The coffin was lowered very deep beneath the white chalk that had been turned up close to the church walls. We said good-bye to him and came back to the Bridge that he has crossed for the last time. No Lethe flowed beneath those glimmering arches. Every wave will echo with his memory as long as or racing-oar blades stir the current of the stream he loved. The fog that strangled that brave heart had left us. The sky was clear above our heads. He, too, had passed out of the darkness into light.

Letters continued in 20 and 27 November, at which point the magazine explained that,

> We must now reluctantly refuse, from lack of space, any further contributions and letters on the subject of the late W B Woodgate, whose death has aroused correspondence from a very wide area. A Brasenose friend has forwarded the following –
>
> > Woodgate his name the sylvan gods bestowed,
> > Through BNC, their Brazengate proclaimed him;
> > In many a victory he sculled or rowed,
> > Never a 'passenger' until Charon claimed him.

The Field noted that many similar verses in Greek, Latin and English had been sent. The editor, Cook, quotes an even better 'elegiac couplet' in his own memoirs, that was sent to him by one of Woodgate's 'old friends, a clergyman':

> 'Lignea Porta' vale, Stygias abiture per undias,
> Aurea Porta tibi stet patefacta precor.

> 'Wood Gate' we called you; now you pass before.
> On Stygian streams to wield your well-known oar,
> We send you greeting: may your luck still hold
> Till you pass safely through the Gates of Gold.

There is something appropriate in all this for Vincent's, which remains surrounded by myths. It is difficult to convince believers that some familiar stories are simply untrue or at least embellished. In 1964, for instance, an American newspaper reported under the headline 'That Vincent's Tie Circles The Earth' (with a note 'including Russia') an apocryphal story of a Vincent's member who arrived in Moscow having forgotten his passport being waved through immigration by a Soviet official who recognised the tie. The newspaper endeared itself to members by explaining:

> That necktie, dark blue silk dotted with silver crowns is one of the most coveted pieces of apparel in the world. It usually signifies that the owner is an athlete of international standing, for Vincent's Club skims the cream from Oxford's sporting world.

Quite so, but the story has no means of identification or verification and is implausible. As Wenden has taught us in film, however, there might be a kind of truth conveyed by fiction. The Vincent's tie is indeed a significant factor in the enduring appeal of lifelong membership of this extraordinary Club.

A very powerful myth is that Harold Macmillan was a member when he was an undergraduate before the First World War, despite having no particular interest in sport. This never seemed plausible to those who have a copy of the 1964 list of members which dates his membership to 1963, not to 50 years earlier. It has been difficult to convince people, however, that Macmillan's membership has been read back into history from an honorary membership conferred in the centenary year when he was invited to address Vincent's celebratory dinner. One of many biographical and autobiographical accounts of his earlier life has a photograph of a Balliol reading-party in the Alps in 1913. Macmillan's comment is that 'I don't remember the name of the athletic man next to me wearing a Rowing Blue's jersey and cricket boots; I think he was killed in the First War'.

As the Club unearths records, not least in preparing for the refurbishment of the current premises, a definitive answer might soon materialise as to whether Macmillan's fellow Balliol student, the great pre-World War I rugby player, Ronnie Poulton was invited to become a member of Vincent's. If so, it seems that he did not frequent the Club. Would Macmillan really have become a member if Poulton were not? In April 2013, as the Club prepared for its refurbishment, a minute-book was found in the attic. On 2 October 1962, it records that, 'The committee then moved on to the election of new members. The first under consideration was a proposal by post that the Vice-Chancellor [sic, he was the Chancellor] of the University, The Rt Hon Harold Macmillan, should be an honorary member.' After a short discussion, he was elected. Joe McPartlin signed the minutes. The tie might have been handed over at the 1963 dinner or the membership is dated from that occasion because of its significance. In other news from the same committee meeting, Walter's had agreed to experiment with a batch of ties with an extra row of crowns.

In the complete set of membership lists for the 19th century there is no mention of some great sportsmen from that era, such as Cuthbert Ottaway, Sir Theodore Cook or Sir Pelham Warner. Cook and Warner have written about eating in Vincent's and being there, which is not quite the same as having been members. In the 20th century, the ice hockey varsity player, Prime Minister of Canada and Nobel Peace Laureate, Lester 'Mike' Pearson, does not seem to have been a member, and another disappointment is that there is no record thus far of the American Eddie Eagan joining the Club, despite his fame as one of those rare Olympians to win a gold medal in both the summer and winter Games, in boxing and bobsleigh respectively. Likewise, the greatest cricketer in Oxford and Pakistan's history and a rising politician, Imran Khan, does not figure on membership lists, even if his photo held a prominent position on the wall of the Club's bar, near The Beatles (who were not members either).

Of those who demonstrably were members, any other author might have chosen different characters for his preferred vignettes of Vincent's. Others might have concentrated on the physical premises, the moves within a short span of Oxford's High Street and just around one of its corners. Many believe that the genius of the Club is in its stewards, some in its senior members. Again, the photos on the walls of the bar show the esteem in which both sets of contributors to the ethos of Vincent's are held. The current team of chef, barman and bursar/administrator are impressive characters. It has been a tradition to call the front-of-house person by name, usually John, whether or not that was their given name. The current incumbent, Lenny, is unfailingly cheerful, efficient and helpful, knowing each member by face and name.

Indeed, some think that the photos on the walls themselves play a large part in creating the atmosphere, with the occasional memento, item of memorabilia, team list or plaque. There are tributes to Airey Neave and Bob Nairac, for instance, on the walls of the bar, both of whom were killed by terrorists. But as the country prepares to mark the centenaries of all the significant stages of the First World War, it is timely that the Club's refurbishment and perhaps the stimulus of this introduction to its history prompts the current members to think about recalling also some of the other pioneers, heroes and high-flyers whose lives have been touched upon in these pages.

Others again might imagine that the heart of the Club is in the committee meetings. Yet the minutes, or notes, of meetings show a preoccupation with food, the cost of food, the quality of food, whether Hawk's or the Pitt Club should be the reciprocal club in Cambridge, the disappearance of tankards (for instance after Cardiff rugby football club had visited), the gradual reappearance or replacement of tankards, the cost of membership, the deficit, dances, cocktail parties, photographs, dinners, re-covering of chairs, re-laying of stair carpets, and whether to invest in a television set. Any rows over membership have not been recorded, although the criteria for membership, the process of election and the purposes of the Club have been set out in successive constitutions. The new constitution begins with admirable clarity in setting out the purposes of Vincent's:

The objects of the Club shall be:

(a) To promote excellence in all sport activities available to student members of the University of Oxford …

(b) To apply the funds and other property of the Club … in pursuance of the above objective and in providing a venue and facilities for meetings of members of the Club.

(c) To collaborate, where practicable, with Atalanta's Club in achieving (a) above and to foster social ties with members of Atalanta's Club.

Atalanta's Club could be described as a sister club to Vincent's. It was established at the beginning of this century by and for sportswomen who have won Blues or half-Blues. How the clubs decide to develop, whether in partnership as distinct entities or in ever-closer union, will be a fascinating part of the next 50 years. W B Woodgate founded Vincent's in the century before women could be members of the University of Oxford, so there was no explicit ban on them in his first set of rules, merely a silence caused by the impossibility of women becoming Oxford students in 1863. In his *Reminiscences* in 1909, Woodgate showed that he was not one who always believed that sport was better in the good old days. He also welcomed the advent of sportswomen:

> To sum up; I am forced to the conclusion that sport is far healthier morally, and also at a higher standard, than it was when I was first initiated into various branches of it. One feature which I acclaim is the initiation of ladies into many branches of it which would have horrified duennas of my boyhood, who regarded embroidery, music and painting as the duties of their charges: and would have regarded feminine equitation without a groom – or a damsel hunting – as qualification for divorce or demi-monde: the like as to any girl who handled the ribbons; while lawn-tennis, golf, or swimming would have been voted by them as only fit for barmaids. I do not see that feminine tone has been depreciated by this emancipation from former thraldom of Mrs Grundy.

Rather than end on the question for members of the future constitution of the Club, it seems appropriate in a year of celebration, and bearing in mind John Buchan's warnings against grand conclusions, to round off this introduction to Vincent's with the more mundane but perennially preoccupying questions of food and fun. In this 150th anniversary year, the Club has already held 'decade' dinners, bringing together alumni such as the president of 1980, Reg Clark, already mentioned, and a rugby player he had played against and stayed with when Oxford played Edinburgh on tour. Andrew Widdowson was treasurer of his undergraduate university rugby club, came to Oxford to train as a teacher, was seriously injured in a college rugby game in 1980, breaking his back, spent months at Stoke Mandeville, was elected to Vincent's and has taught at Felsted, coached rugby from his wheelchair and directed the school's arts festival for decades, appearing in newspapers shortly after his spinal injury for being invited to the royal wedding of 1981, having previously escorted Lady Diana Spencer to the Argyll Ball. Reuniting opponents and fellow Vincent's men in conversation is at the heart of the Club's commitment to lifelong membership.

In an earlier chapter, the story was told of another injured rugby player (and cricketer), Duke Hussey, facing death and being saved by the doctor he had met at Vincent's bar. Hussey wrote to Girdlestone, who invited the war hero to lunch and then carried out a series of pioneering operations on him, at the end of his own medical career. J C Masterman knew the doctor and explains the great man's explanation of the meaning of life, as seen from the perspective of a golfer:

> Gathorne Girdlestone, the great surgeon, with whom I played much, seemed to me to have the root of the matter in him. 'When you have a critical putt to hole it is the most important thing in the world; after you have missed it nothing could matter less.' So he told me once and after his retirement he wrote to me to suggest that we should play regularly, 'just you and I, proper fierce happy singles, lots of fun and friendship and the rigour of the game'.

There is a view that none of us would be here were it not for the duplicity of Masterman the spymaster. We have already seen that he could be a spiteful opponent, as when he took against Vincent's most scholarly FA Cup winner, Arthur Johnson. But he also took something of the Club's spirit into his important war work. At the same time as he was chairing the XX Committee, it will be recalled, he was attending Vincent's committee meetings. In Christopher Andrew's magisterial book *The Defence of the Realm*, the authorised history of MI5, he says that

> As well as being an academic, Masterman was probably the best all-round games player ever to join the Security Service. As an undergraduate he had won an

athletics Blue. Between the wars he played hockey and tennis for England and at the age of forty-six was still a good enough cricketer to tour Canada with the MCC. In his reports on the Double-Cross System, Masterman sometimes used cricketing analogies. 'Running a team of double agents', he believed, 'is very like running a club cricket side. Older players lose their form and are gradually replaced by newcomers.' He compared the leading double agents to well-known cricketers: 'If in the double-cross world SNOW was the W G Grace of the early period, then GARBO was certainly the Bradman of the later years ... Masterman was also an excellent chairman. He preceded the first meeting of the Twenty Committee with what he later called a small but important decision, to wit that tea and a bun should always be provided for members. In days of acute shortage and of rationing the provision of buns was no easy task, yet by hook or crook (and mostly by crook) we never failed to provide them throughout the war years. Was this simple expedient one of the reasons why attenance at the Committee was nearly always a hundred per cent?'

Christopher Andrew reports that, despite the obvious conflicts between spymasters, Masterman's chairing and his gift for achieving consensus in this committee meant that 'At only one of its 226 meetings was a disagreement pressed to a vote'. Food features frequently in the otherwise minimalist fragments of records of Vincent's but it does so as nourishing what is important, namely that ethos of fellowship. In the minutes of Vincent's committee meeting of Sunday 24 April 1949, consensus was reached on a most important matter which was entrusted to the archetypal Vincent's member (and later president):

The question of a Cold Buffet table was left in the hands of Mr R G Bannister, the Committee being in general agreement that such a proposal be implemented.

Sources

Selected sources are listed in order of chapter content.

Chapter 1: The Founder

W B Woodgate, *Reminiscences of an Old Sportsman*, Eveleigh Nash, 1909

Sir Theodore Cook, *Character & Sportsmanship*, William Norgate, 1927

F E Weatherly KC, *Piano and Gown,* Putnam, 1926

G C Drinkwater and T R B Saunders, *The University Boat Race Official Centenary History*, Cassell, 1929

Christopher Dodd, *The Oxford and Cambridge Boat Race*, Hutchinson, 1983

Chapter 2: The Pioneers

The on-line resources of the Achilles Club and of Oxford University Athletics Club have been especially helpful. Graham Tanner's history of OUAC deserves the highest praise: http://www.ouac.org/wp-content/uploads/2012/05/history.pdf

M G Brock and M C Curthoys (editors), *The History of the University of Oxford*, Vol VII, *Nineteenth Century, Part 2*, OUP, 2000, Ch 22 H S Jones, 'University and College Sport'

Howard Marshall, *Oxford v Cambridge, The Story of the University Rugby Match*, Clarke & Cockeran, 1951

George Chesterton and Hubert Doggart, *Oxford and Cambridge Cricket*, Collins, 1989

P F Warner and F S Ashley-Cooper, *Oxford v Cambridge at the Wicket*, Allen & Unwin, 1926

David Frost, *The Bowring Story of the Varsity Match*, Macdonald Queen Anne Press, 1988

Colin Weir, *The History of the Oxford University Association Football Club 1872–1998*, Yore Publications, 1998

Keith Warsop, *The Early FA Cup Finals and the Southern Amateurs*, SoccerData, 2004

Hartwell de la Garde Grissell, *Sede Vacante*, James Parker, 1903

Guy Nickalls, *Life's a Pudding*, Faber, 1939

D Batchelor, *C B Fry*, Phoenix House, 1951

Clive Ellis, *C B: The Life of Charles Burgess Fry*, Dent, 1984

Jeremy Malies, *Sporting Doubles*, Robson, 1998

G D 'Khaki' Roberts QC, *Without My Wig*, Macmillan, 1957

Thérèse Radic (editor), *Race against Time: The Diaries of F S Kelly 1907–1915*, National Library of Australia, 2004

F S Kelly, chapter on 'Sculling', in R C Lehmann, *The Complete Oarsman*, Methuen, 1908 https://archive.org/details/completeoarsman00lehmgoog

Sir Edward Grey, *Fly-Fishing*, 1899, 1907 fourth edition, Dent & Co

Chapter 3: The Heroes

The National Archives on-line provide citations for all the Military Cross and Victoria Cross awards.

Brian Harrison (editor), *The History of the University of Oxford, Volume 8, The Twentieth-Century*, OUP, 1994, Ch 20, D C Wenden, 'Sports'

G M Trevelyan, *Grey of Fallodon*, Longman, 1937

J C Masterman, *On the Chariot Wheel*, OUP, 1975

Lord Home, *The Way the Wind Blows*, Collins, 1976

Julie Summers, *Fearless of Everest, the Quest for Sandy Irvine*, Phoenix, 2000

Prince Alex Obolensky, 'Through God – The Renaissance of Russia', in Keith Briant and George Joseph (editors), *Be Still and Know*, Michael Joseph, 1936, pp101–20

E W Swanton, *Last Over*, Richard Cohen, London, 1996

John Lewes, *Jock Lewes: Co-Founder of the SAS*, Leo Cooper, 2000

Marmaduke Hussey, *Chance Governs All*, Macmillan, 2002

Sir Thomas Macpherson, *Behind Enemy Lines*, Mainstream, 2012

Roger Bannister, *First Four Minutes*, Putnam, 1955

D J Wenden, *Battleship Potemkin: Film and Reality*, in K M R Short (editor), *Feature Films as History*, Croom Helm, 1981

Clive van Ryneveld, *20th Century All-Rounder*, PreText, 2011

J C Masterman, *The Double-Cross System in the war of 1939 to 1945*, Yale, 1972

Derek Johnson, 'Losing an Olympic Title', in Chris Brasher (editor), *The Road to Rome*, William Kimber, 1960, pp27–34

Chapter 4: The High-Flyers

www.cricketarchive.com is comprehensive for scorecards.

Jan Morris, *Oxford*, OUP, 1965

Sir Keith Feiling, *In Christ Church Hall*, Macmillan, 1960

Blanche d'Alpuget, *Robert J Hawke, a Biography*, Penguin, 1994

Daniel Topolski with Patrick Robinson, *True Blue, The Oxford Boat Race Mutiny*, Doubleday, 1989

Alison Gill, *The Yanks at Oxford, the 1987 Boat Race Controversy*, Book Guild, 1991

Graham Richards, *50 Years at Oxford*, 2011, AuthorHouse

Tony Pawson, *Runs & Catches*, Faber, 1980

Chapter 5: Against the Current

W Thesiger, *Arabian Sands*, Penguin, 2007

John Buchan, *Brasenose College*, F E Robinson, 1898

C Andrew, *The Defence of the Realm, The Authorized History of MI5*, Allen Lane, 2008

'That Vincent's Tie Circles the Earth' http://news.google.com/newspapers?nid=1842&-dat=19640818&id=5hMsAAAAIBAJ&sjid=iMY-EAAAAIBAJ&pg=3940,5576086

List of Presidents

1863	Walter Bradford Woodgate	*Brasenose*
1863	C Ellis	*Merton*
1864	C W Spencer-Stanhope	*Merton*
1865	J H Forster	*University*
1865	Edward Carr Glyn	*University*
1866	W H Jenkins	*Merton*
1866	Albert Brassey	*University*
1867	Lansdowne, Marquis of	*Balliol*
1868	W Wightman Wood	*University*
1868	Edward L Fellowes	*Brasenose*
1869	S H Woodhouse	*University*
1870	J C Tinne	*University*
1871	C S Newton	*University*
1872	Robert Lesley	*Pembroke*
1872	W Townsend	*Brasenose*
1873	E S Garnier	*University*
1874	M G Farrer	*Brasenose*
1875	W Walter Whitmore	*Brasenose*
1876	J G Bankes	*University*
1876	Chesterfield, Lord	*Brasenose*
1877	T C Edwards-Moss	*Brasenose*
1878	Audley C Miles	*Brasenose*
1879	W H Cross	*University*
1879	W H Grenfell (later Lord Desborough)	
		Balliol
1880	G D Rowe	*University*
1881	A H Evans	*Oriel*
1881	J Lubbock	*Balliol*
1882	W W Palmer, Hon	
	(later Earl of Selborne)	*University*
1882	Brinsley Fitzgerald	*University*
1883	A R Paterson	*Trinity*
1884	M C Kemp	*Hertford*
1885	A G Asher	*Brasenose*
1885	L Owen	*New*
1886	D H McLean	*New*
1886	H T Arnold-Thompson	*Brasenose*

1887	G W Ricketts	*Oriel*
1887	H H Castens	*Brasenose*
1888	H R Parker	*Brasenose*
1889	H Philipson	*New*
1890	Guy Nickalls	*Magdalen*
1891	F Thesiger	*Magdalen*
1892	Edward Murray	*Oriel*
1893	Encombe, Lord	*Magdalen*
1894	Hugh B Cotton	*Magdalen*
1895	W Burton Stewart	*Brasenose*
1896	Henry D G Leveson-Gower	*Magdalen*
1897	E R Balfour	*University*
1898	C K Philips	*New*
1899	Thomas A Nelson	*University*
1900	R E 'Tip' Foster	*University*
1901	Felix W Warre	*Balliol*
1902	Horace J Hale	*Balliol*
1903	W Findlay	*Oriel*
1904	E G Monier-Williams	*University*
1905	A K Graham	*Balliol*
1906	K Cornwallis	*University*
1907	Patrick Munro	*Christ Church*
1908	E L Wright	*New*
1909	A G Kirby	*Magdalen*
1910	H Bonsey	*University*
1911	G Cunningham	*Magdalen*
1912	R O Lagden	*Oriel*
1913	Roy Bardsley	*Merton*
1914	D M Bain	*Trinity*
1915–18	H le B Lightfoot (Snr Treasurer)	
		Corpus Christi
1919	Edward D Horsfall	*Magdalen*
1920	Miles Howell	*Oriel*
1921	Bevil G D'U Rudd	*Trinity*
1922	V R Price	*Magdalen*
1923	W R Milligan	*University*
1924	R J Denison	*Oriel*

1925	H J Kittermaster	*University*		1969	R H Phillips	*Corpus Christi*
1926	Dunglass	*Christ Church*		1969	F S Goldstein	*St Edmund Hall*
1927	G E B Abell	*Corpus Christi*		1970	J L Corbett	*St Peter's*
1928	Charles Frazer	*Balliol*		1971	P R Carroll	*Mansfield*
1929	D A Nunn	*New*		1972	G B Stevenson	*University*
1930	A T Barber	*Queen's*		1973	C B Hamblin	*Keble*
1931	J S M Paul	*St John's*		1974/5	J W Lee	*Christ Church*
1932	P G V van der Bijl	*Brasenose*		1975/6	P N A Quinnen	*Wadham*
1933	Alan McWillis	*Trinity*		1977	R I Eddington	*Lincoln*
1934	J E Lovelock	*Exeter*		1978	P B Fisher	*Christ Church*
1935	Michael Mosley	*Trinity*		1979	J G M Webster	*Oriel*
1936	John W Seamer	*Brasenose*		1980	R B Clark	*Christ Church*
1937	Roger Pulbrook	*Magdalen*		1981	J J Rogers	*University*
1938	Alan Pennington	*Hertford*		1982	R Marsden	*Christ Church*
1939	F M M Forster	*Trinity*		1983	A H Hobart	*Exeter*
1940	J C Lawrie (Hon Sec)	*Brasenose*		1984	P B Mbu	*St Edmund Hall*
1941	R C H Risley (Hon Sec)	*Oriel*		1985	A J T Miller	*St Edmund Hall*
1942	E K Scott (Hon Sec)	*Lincoln*		1986	C S Horner	*Worcester*
1943	W J H Butterfield (Hon Sec)	*Exeter*		1987	J M Risman	*St Edmund Hall*
1944	D A B Garton-Sprenger			1988	M Lawson-Statham	*University*
	(Hon Sec)	*Merton*		1989	D J Bucknall	*St Peter's*
1945	J B Dossetor (Hon Sec)	*St John's*		1990	R J Horrocks-Taylor	*St Peter's*
1946	David Macindoe MC	*Christ Church*		1991	M Merrick	*Christ Church*
1947	David G Jamison	*Magdalen*		1992	S Sparrow	*St Edmund Hall*
1948	J O Newton-Thompson	*Trinity*		1993	J R Elliot	*St Anne's*
1949	G P Jackson	*Brasenose*		1994	T Watson	*St Edmund Hall*
1950	Roger G Bannister	*Exeter*		1995	A N S Bryce	*St Edmund Hall*
1951	D B Carr	*Worcester*		1996	A D O'Mahony	*St Anne's*
1952	P D S Blake	*Brasenose*		1997	A T Roberts-Miller	*Worcester*
1953	C S Cheshire	*Trinity*		1998	T G A Griffiths	*Keble*
1954	R K Pitamber	*St Edmund Hall*		1999	J P Willcocks	*Brasenose*
1955	D C P R Jowett	*St John's*		2000	T A Doyle	*St Edmund Hall*
1955	Roy C P Allaway	*University*		2001	R G Woodfine	*St Edmund Hall*
1956	M J K Smith	*St Edmund Hall*		2002	T O R Perry	*St Edmund Hall*
1957	D J N Johnson	*Lincoln*		2003	J J Fulford	*Worcester*
1958	Robin H Davies	*New*		2004	C T T Edwards	*Balliol*
1959	Mike A Eagar	*Worcester*		2005	D G Hughes	*Jesus*
1960	A W N Gemmill	*Brasenose*		2006	J P E Boto	*University*
1961	F E Robin Butler	*University*		2007	D N Abbott	*Somerville*
1962	I L Elliott	*Keble*		2008	R W H Payne	*St Peter's*
1963	J J McPartlin	*St Edmund Hall*		2009	T D Smith	*Worcester*
1964	C J G Atkinson	*St Edmund Hall*		2010	H A McCormick	*Lincoln*
1965	J M W Hogan	*Trinity*		2011	A J Healy	*Worcester*
1966	M R J Guest	*Magdalen*		2012	J A Pearson-Stuttard	*Christ Church*
1967	R M Oliver	*St Edmund Hall*		2013	B R Mansfield	*Oriel*
1968	G N S Ridley	*Pembroke*		2014	M A Neil	*St Hilda's*

Index